THE BATTLE OF AMIENS
1918

and Operations 8th August - 3rd September, 1918

The Turn of the Tide on the Western Front

WITH
FIVE MAPS

BY

A. KEARSEY, D.S.O., O.B.E., *p.s.c.*

LATE LIEUTENANT-COLONEL, GENERAL STAFF

Author of
MARLBOROUGH'S CAMPAIGNS
THE AMERICAN CIVIL WAR
MESOPOTAMIA CAMPAIGN, 1914-17
GALLIPOLI CAMPAIGN
1915 CAMPAIGN IN FRANCE
EGYPT AND PALESTINE CAMPAIGN, 1914-17 (2 vols.)
etc. etc.

ALDERSHOT
GALE & POLDEN LIMITED
1950

First Published February, 1950

CONTENTS

DATES OF PRINCIPAL EVENTS

INTRODUCTION

This period covers thirty-two fighting days—Reference to Second Marne battle starting 15th July, 1918, to indicate drain on Ludendorff's resources—Comparison with the plans of Generalissimo Foch—Continuance of offensive beyond original objectives on the Chemin des Dames, with costly results to Ludendorff's own reserves—Successful local attacks delivered by British during June and July showed that Germans had not strongly built up newly won defences—Ludendorff did not anticipate Allied attack on Château-Thierry—Reims salient—Foch enabled to start offensive at 4.20 a.m. on 8th August with every prospect of success—Discussion as to Foch's methods later of delivering a series of blows in rapid succession at different and converging points.

CHAPTER I

APPRECIATION OF THE SITUATION, 1st AUGUST, 1918

1.—OBJECT TO BE ATTAINED

To carry out a mobile offensive combined with the element of surprise by striking a series of blows at unexpected points where the enemy's reserves were not at hand—Comparison of methods of German General Staff, who carried out attacks until the defenders were able to stabilize their lines under diminishing pressure—Foch, on the other hand, would strike until the enemy's resistance hardened and their reserves had been brought in; he then would stop the advance and attack elsewhere before the enemy could foresee the direction of the new advance—Long wait for Foch, as since 21st March, 1918, Ludendorff had the initiative.

2.—FACTORS AFFECTING THE ATTAINMENT OF THE OBJECT

Details of opposing forces on 8th August, 1918—Strength of the Allies enormously enhanced by the appointment of a great commander, namely, Ferdinand Foch, as Commander-in-Chief—His character analysed, with a tribute to his outstanding qualities and his trained instinct for war—His patience in waiting for his opportunity until 18th July—Situation at the end of April, when we were standing with our backs to the wall, when Haig's army of forty-five divisions and three cavalry divisions had checked the attacks of a hundred and nine German divisions—Foch fortunate in having a loyal, resolute British commander with high military talent as his chief adviser—Ludendorff, in spite of methodical care in planning, was definitely defeated

iii

on 29th April by the skilful use of reserves created by Foch's daring policy of drawing troops from quiet areas to vital points—Situation when the army of the Crown Prince had reached the Marne in June, and had driven a salient into our front to Château-Thierry between Soissons and Reims—Use made by Ludendorff of the 207 divisions on Western Front—Decided he could confidently undertake a fourth offensive and link up the two salients by the capture of Compiègne—Use of fourteen divisions of the Crown Prince Rupprecht's reserves intended for his final phase—They were employed in Second Marne battle—American troops and forces from Salonika and Palestine now appearing in the forward lines—Successful local attacks delivered by our Second Army on 28th June at La Becques, by General Byng, north-west of Albert, and by the 9th Division near Meteren—Ludendorff further decreased his reserves in June for his attack on Compiègne—Difficult decision for Foch, as enemy might use their reserves either to strike towards the Channel ports or towards Paris—In the middle of July, when Ludendorff was ready to attack, he had a great superiority in man power, but overlooked in his calculation the value of tanks.

Australian Corps, with sixty tanks, on 4th July captured Hamel and 1,500 prisoners—Ludendorff's plan for his operations on 15th July explained—No diversion and no attempt to draw off the Allies' reserves—Germans' advance across the Marne unsupported by artillery—Noon on 16th July, Ludendorff ordered the suspension of the offensive by the First and Third Armies and the organization of the defence—Critical situation for German troops south of the River Marne.

Ludendorff's dilemma as to further advance across the Marne, to leave troops on the southern bank or continue the offensive north of this river—He now left this vital area to confer with the Crown Prince Rupprecht—Foch always on the spot where vital decisions had to be made—22nd July an order was given for the withdrawal of troops in the southern part of the salient—Already 25,000 prisoners and 400 guns had been captured—Safety for Ludendorff now depended on his ability to build up a new reserve as soon as possible—Plan for 8th August for an offensive battle by three corps and 420 fighting tanks and No. 8 Squadron, R.A.F.

CHAPTER II

EVENTS LEADING UP TO THE BATTLE OF AMIENS,
8TH AUGUST, 1918

Germans ordered a withdrawal in the River Lys plain and from Ancre and Avre bridgeheads—On 6th August the 27th German Division attacked on the front planned for our attack on 8th August—Arrangements made for security and surprise for 8th August, Battle of Amiens.

Details of the course of operations for 8th August—Namely, for the enemy to be driven out of range of Amiens and the Paris railway—On reaching the old Amiens defence line there was to be exploitation up to the old British front line—French corps starting forty-five minutes after zero on our right was to maintain contact with the Canadian Corps.

CHAPTER III

THE FIRST DAY OF THE BATTLE OF AMIENS

CONSIDERED FROM THE POINT OF VIEW OF THE APPLICATION OF THE PRINCIPLES OF WAR

1. Surprise was gained by secrecy, by calculated deception and stratagem and unsuspected weight and direction of the attack east of Amiens—Result was continuous success by Australian and Canadian Corps in fighting their way forward—Canadian Corps, co-operating with Australian Corps, gained some fifty square miles and captured 5,000 prisoners and 161 guns; the Australian Corps captured thirty square miles and nearly 8,000 prisoners and 173 guns; the III Corps captured 600 prisoners—Ludendorff considered that counter-attack with his decreasing reserves was impossible on a large scale—Ludendorff's opinion on the result of the fighting on 8th August—Arranged conferences with the Imperial Chancellor to discuss peace questions.

CHAPTER IV

BATTLE OF AMIENS FROM 9TH AUGUST, 1918

Main advance to be made by the Canadian Corps with the French on their right and the Australians on their left to cover their flanks—Substantial progress was made on 9th August, but we were short of our objectives—On 10th August the German resistance stiffened—British Commander-in-Chief now started to complete details of plans for capture of La Bassée and Aubers Ridge by the First Army—German resistance increased—The Commander-in-Chief decided now to strike from the Albert-Arras front through Bapaume to dislocate Ludendorff's plans for retreat—Results of the Battle of Amiens summarized—The Generalissimo decided to strike before the enemy could retire in their own time—On 17th August the French Tenth Army attacked between the Oise and the Aisne against the German Ninth Army—Ludendorff then became engaged on the front between the Avre and the Vesle.

CHAPTER V

OPERATIONS FROM 21ST AUGUST

Haig's aim was by a limited advance to recover the Arras-Albert railway and later to deliver a general attack north of the River Somme—The Third Army started the attack at 4.55 a.m. on 21st August on a front of nine miles—By the evening our advance was up to three miles along the Albert-Arras railway—On the 22nd the III Australian Corps came into action between Albert and the River Somme with similar success—Von Boehn was now withdrawing to the south bank of the River Oise—On the 23rd the Third and Fourth Armies on a thirty-three-mile front made steady progress—We won a footing on the Thiepval Ridge and the Third Army was astride the Arras-Bapaume road and closing in on Bapaume from the north—On the 24th the whole Thiepval Ridge was cleared—On the 25th we captured Mametz, Martinpuich and Le Sars—On the 27th the French captured Roye—Von Boehn was in full retreat between Roye and the Oise—By the 28th the French had pushed on nine miles to the Upper Somme.

CHAPTER VI

BATTLE OF THE RIVER SCARPE

At 3 a.m. on 26th August the First Army attacked on a five-mile front astride the River Scarpe—We won in one day as much as we had gained in six weeks in this area in the 1917 Arras battle—On 27th August Roeux and Gavrelle were captured—In the past seven days we had taken 26,000 prisoners—Ludendorff's reserves were shrinking—On 29th August von Boehn was retreating to a position on the Ailette, Oise, Upper Somme and Tortille—Combles, Morval and Bapaume fell on 29th August—Road to Cambrai now open to the advance of the Third Army—On the 30th the First Army was in touch with the Drocourt-Quéant Switch—Farther south we took Bancourt and Vaulx-Vraucourt—At 5 a.m. on the 31st the 5th Australian Brigade, by a dashing exploit, captured Mt. St. Quentin, commanding Péronne, which was entered on 1st September—In Flanders we retook Bailleul station—Ludendorff's intermediate position was untenable—On 2nd September the Fourth Army advanced east of Péronne, the Third Army was behind Bullecourt, and at 5 a.m. the First Army and three divisions of the Third Army astride the Arras-Cambrai road attacked the Drocourt-Quéant position—Six miles of this position and 8,000 prisoners were captured—On 3rd September the Fourth Army and French army on its right crossed the River Somme—In Flanders we had recovered Neuve Chapelle and the front ran from Voormezeele to Ploegsteert—By 4th September the enemy were in position on the east side of the Canal du Nord from the Scarpe to the River Tortille—Preparation now was to be made for the last series of battles, for which Foch had been preparing for final victory.

CHAPTER VII

NOTES FOR SOLUTION OF QUESTIONS—TWELVE QUESTIONS WITH ANSWERS

MAPS

SUMMARY

MAPS AT END OF BOOK

MAP 1.—SITUATION, 7TH AUGUST, 1918.

MAP 2.—ADVANCE ON 8TH AUGUST, 1918, BY FOURTH ARMY AND FIRST FRENCH ARMY.

MAP 3.—ADVANCE OF THIRD ARMY, 21ST TO 23RD AUGUST, 1918.

MAP 4.—FOURTH ARMY ADVANCE, 27TH TO 29TH AUGUST, 1918.

MAP 5.—ADVANCE, 30TH AUGUST TO 4TH SEPTEMBER, 1918, BY THIRD AND FIRST ARMIES.

DATES OF PRINCIPAL EVENTS

18th July to 6th August . The Second Battle of the Marne.

6th August . . . . Action south of Morlancourt.

8th August . . . . Battles of Amiens and Montdidier.

11th August . . . . End of Battle of Amiens.

15th August . . . . End of Battle of Montdidier.

17th August . . . . Battle of Noyon.

18th August . . . . Advance in Flanders.
Action at Outtersteene.

21st August . . . . Battle of Albert.

22nd August . . . . Battle of the Scarpe.

27th August . . . . German retirement to the Somme Line
started. Bapaume captured.
End of Battles of Noyon and Albert.

30th August . . . . End of Battle of the Scarpe.
Second Battle of Bapaume begins.

31st August . . . . Evacuation of Mt. Kemmel.

1st September . . . Péronne and Mt. St. Quentin captured.

2nd September . . . Battle of Drocourt-Quéant.

2nd September . . . Retirement to Hindenburg positions
begins.

3rd September . . . Second Battle of Bapaume ends.
Occupation of Lens.

FOREWORD

THE author's qualifications are that for many years he has given detailed attention to the progress of military science in addition to the study of military history.

The author has endeavoured to make comments on the operations and situations with judgment and impartiality following the principles of war which are advocated in our official manuals.

1915 CAMPAIGN IN FRANCE

"Ce livre nous donne un exposé fidèle et précis de trois opérations offensives."

BIBLIOGRAPHIE FRANCAISE.

INTRODUCTION

THIS account covers a period of thirty-two important days of fighting on the Western Front in 1918.

Reference has also been made to the Second Marne battle in July, as it has an important bearing on the offensive operations starting on 8th August, 1918. It was thought necessary to show how this battle developed into such a drain on Ludendorff's man power and re- sources that late in July he was forced to relinquish his plans for launching his final stroke for victory owing to the exhaustion of his reserves in the preliminaries for it. Consistently he had been prosecu- ting the offensives as he did on the Chemin des Dames, starting on 29th May beyond the original objectives with costly results to his reserves, which must be difficult to replenish. The German gains, in fact, were obtained at such a heavy price that long intervals were necessary to prepare for succeeding blows. The initial success by the Germans was thus a misfortune to their commander, whose judgment in continuing the offensive in one direction was tested to his own undoing.

He lost sight of the battlefront as a whole, and the value of main- taining as intact as possible a powerful fighting reserve. Successful local attacks were delivered during June and July on the British front. These indicated that the Germans had not strongly built up their newly won defence lines, and that their morale was not equal at all times to the strain of surprise attacks. Ludendorff, finally, by not anticipating the Allied attack on the Château-Thierry—Reims salient, enabled Foch to start his offensive operations at 4.20 a.m. on 8th August, 1918, with every prospect of success. Now the Generalissimo had at last, after long waiting, gained his opportunity. The tide had turned in his favour; the enemy had drawn too heavily on reserves; so that he had wrested the initiative from the German commander. This little account could not have been written without reference to Volume IV of the British Official History, in which, as usual, the details are marshalled and the essentials are emphasized with the skill and clarity of the preceding volumes.

That this volume is most strongly recommended for a wider study of this interesting period of the 1914-18 war goes without saying. The great interest in the study of the operations in this official volume lies not only in the fact that at last victory was in sight but in the comparison of the methods of the opposing commanders. This is most instructive. It is clearly shown that Ludendorff carried his slowly staged divergent attacks beyond the limits of profitable exploitation at the time when he had a preponderance of force, and when consequently the initiative was his.

Our very great Generalissimo, Ferdinand Foch, on the other hand, delivered a series of blows in rapid succession at different points in order to mystify the enemy, and make him direct his reserves to places dictated by his own plan of operations. The Editor of the Official History points out that there were finally on the Allied side a "series of attacks following each other closely at different places."

Ludendorff soon after the decisive battle of 8th August felt that he must confess "that leadership had assumed the character of an irresponsible game of chance, and that the war must be ended."

CHAPTER I

APPRECIATION OF THE SITUATION, 1st AUGUST, 1918

1.—OBJECT TO BE ATTAINED

To carry out a mobile offensive combined with the element of surprise. A series of blows were to be struck at unexpected points, at which the enemy had not adequate reserves in hand.

Before the necessary strength could be prepared the enemy would be subjected to heavy losses in men, material and ground by superior forces collected at the decisive spot chosen for the attack on the Allied front.

Thus the enemy's areas of manœuvre would constantly be reduced in efforts to stem the Allied advance or to fill up gaps created by unexpected offensive action. It had been noted by the Generalissimo that the battles on this front up to this time had been of a stereotyped nature. An attack once it was planned by the German General Staff had been carried out until the defenders were able to stabilize their line again after great losses on both sides without any decisive result. The attackers did not move their reserves or change their plans and communications once they were set on a definite line of attack. The losses for the attacker became astronomic and gradually their depleted forces came to a halt, when their enemy were, under diminishing pressure, able to restore their forward positions and communications.

Foch did not intend to repeat our plans and tactics of the attacks on the Somme, at Arras or at Passchendaele.

His object now was to strike as hard as possible in one direction, which threatened one of the enemy's vital communications, and as soon as resistance hardened and reserves had been thrown in he would stop the advance, consolidate the positions gained and attack elsewhere as early as possible before the enemy could foresee the weight or direction of the new advance. The Generalissimo Foch had to wait many months for this opportunity to carry through his new plan, as, since 21st March, 1918, Ludendorff had the initiative. The German commander had used his advantage to press forward until his reserves and resources were expended at the points chosen for the attacks and until the initial effects of surprise had been lost, and the battles had been stabilized with such heavy loss on the Somme, the Lys and, more

1

recently, on the River Marne. With the advent of the American armies it would now be possible for Foch to form his mass of manœuvre for the attainment of his object.

2.—FACTORS AFFECTING THE ATTAINMENT OF THE OBJECT

(a) *Strength of the Opposing Forces, 8th August,* 1918

ALLIES

Fourth Army:

I Canadian Corps (1st, 2nd, 3rd and 4th Canadian and 32nd Divisions).

Australian Corps (1st, 2nd, 3rd, 4th and 5th Divisions).

III Corps (12th, 18th, 47th and 58th and American 33rd Divisions).

Cavalry Corps (1st, 2nd and 3rd Cavalry Divisions).

Four hundred and twelve tanks.

One hundred and twenty supply tanks.

Five brigades of Royal Flying Corps.

Eight hundred aircraft.

Eight balloons.

First French Army (twelve divisions):

XXXI Corps.

IX Corps.

X Corps.

XXXV Corps.

II Cavalry Corps.

One thousand one hundred and four aircraft.

GERMANS

Second Army: fourteen divisions, of which four were in reserve. Regiments as posted from north to south:

54th.

27th.

43rd.

108th.

13th.

41st.

117th.

225th.

14th.

192nd.

In reserve:
  243rd.
  107th.
  109th.

Eighteenth Army:
  Fifteen divisions (five in reserve).
  Three hundred and sixty-five aircraft.

The strength of the Allied forces was at this juncture enormously enhanced by the leadership of one of the world's greatest commanders, Ferdinand Foch, who was appointed Generalissimo at the end of March, 1918.

Foch was not only a master of detail, a great student and a scientific military thinker, but he had a trained instinct for war. He was immensely patient in waiting for his opportunity, and then he was prepared to take every justifiable risk to gain the end in view. From 21st March to 18th July, 1918, he had to withstand the enemy's attacks. No fewer than 141 divisions had attacked against the British and French forces when Ludendorff was making desperate efforts to drive a wedge between the French and British armies. By the time that the battles of March and April had ended, we were standing with our backs to the wall; we had lost 70,000 prisoners and 1,000 guns, when Haig's army of forty-five divisions and three cavalry divisions had checked the attacks of 109 German divisions.

Foch was fortunate in having a loyal, resolute British commander with high military talent as his chief adviser. The British Commander-in-Chief, in his turn, was unshaken in his confidence in the Generalissimo, and in the ultimate result of his strategy. More than any other, supported by his army and corps commanders, he made Foch's plans possible. His splendid confidence and skilful handling of difficult situations enabled him to bear the strain after the attack on 21st March until the end of June, when 300,000 Americans started to arrive each month, and when seasoned British troops from the East were available.

Ludendorff, on the other hand, had the gift of planning with method and care. In his attacks in 1918 he was more successful than any other general had been on the Western Front. But he failed to gain complete success either in his first drive for Amiens on 21st March or in his next great attack on the Arras front six days after his main effort had been brought to a standstill on 29th March. Finally, on 29th April, he was definitely defeated with loss by the skilful use of reserves created by Foch's daring policy of anticipating events and drawing troops from quiet areas to the vital points. Ludendorff had, however, by the end of March, almost reached the outskirts of Amiens, his troops had captured Kemmel and menaced Hazebrouck. The army of the Crown Prince had reached the Marne in June, having driven a salient into our front twenty-six miles deep to Château-Thierry and thirty-three miles wide between Soissons and exclusive of Reims.

This was at a time when Ludendorff had 207 divisions on the Western Front.

Foch had, however, by his great generalship, foiled his efforts, and he had deduced from Ludendorff's methods a plan for delivering a series of limited attacks each mutually co-operative until the enemy's reserves were exhausted. He realized that Ludendorff's attacks had not been delivered to be mutually supporting, or so that one attack affected another for the confusion of an opponent in the use of his reserves. There had been pauses between the offensives with much re-grouping and preparation for each fresh attack, so that our reserves could be moved in time to check the advances finally and to inflict heavy casualties, which the German General Staff had not been able to replace. With American reinforcements arriving regularly, Foch was able to build up a reserve, so that Ludendorff's chances of a crushing victory were growing smaller.

However, so greatly did Ludendorff underrate his opponents that he decided that he could confidently undertake a fourth offensive and at any rate reduce the distance to Paris and link up the two salients by the capture of Compiègne. The difference between the com-manders, whose influence on the opposing forces was to be paramount in the forthcoming vital struggle, was clearly marked by their respec-tive plans. Ludendorff had achieved his initial successes during this year most markedly at St. Quentin by his method of infiltration, close support of artillery and by the determined fighting of his speci-ally trained storm troops. But he had evidently not learnt the lesson of the necessity of attacking on more than one front. He was content to allow his battle, which was essentially based on surprise, to con-tinue until there was no longer any possibility of his intention being misunderstood.

He sent his troops forward until they drifted into a stationary battle at one place.

Ludendorff's offensives in May, June and July were to have been only preliminary measures in preparation for a decisive blow. But, as in April on the Lys, success at one point caused him to continue beyond the original limited plan. More troops were employed than he could afford to lose.

Even fourteen divisions of Crown Prince Rupprecht's reserves intended for his final phase were employed in the Second Marne battle, so that Ludendorff was forced to give up his idea of launching it, because he had exhausted his men and resources in minor efforts.

This occurred at a time when we were bringing in troops with which to reconstitute our cadre divisions, and there was a steady flow of American reinforcements.

We had the time available to reconnoitre our weakened divisions, and to strengthen positions to which we had been forced back. Ludendorff, however, owing to the depletion of his available reserves, gave us the breathing space for reorganization, which was to give Foch a balance of tank strength in his favour. Again, when the Germans attacked at the Battle of Matz on 9th June, although they gained an initial success to the west of the salient created by the Chemin des Dames offensive operations up to 12th June, they had lost very heavily, and had been counter-attacked by the French with success.

Their further losses thus incurred appear to have been the cause of more delay in resuming their main offensive.

Troops from Salonika and Palestine were appearing in the forward lines daily, so that the German delay was most encouraging, as were our successful local attacks delivered by General Plumer with the 5th and 31st Divisions on 28th June at La Becques, by General Byng on 30th June north-west of Albert, and by the 9th Division later near Meteren, against recently captured German positions, which had not been consolidated adequately or in depth. There were signs, too, that their morale was deteriorating.

When, again, Ludendorff took the offensive for his attack on Compiègne in June he only decreased the still strong reserves which he had at his disposal. He did not appreciably improve his position in spite of heavy losses. As soon as this attack under von Hutier had been brought to a standstill by Foch's counter-attack, Ludendorff again started another enterprise before the American troops arrived in sufficient numbers. This was to be a stronger attack especially made for the Kaiser's entry into Paris after a march from his grandstand overlooking the River Marne built for him to see his armies start their victorious advance on 15th July, 1918.

Foch at this time had a difficult decision to make, as the enemy might have used their strong reserves in Flanders under the Bavarian Crown Prince to strike towards the Channel ports, and in order to deal with a main blow towards Paris he must draw on the British troops covering these ports. Ludendorff required a full month for this plan to be in working order. During this time reserves were being built up by Foch. They were to be ready at the decisive point owing to his sound forethought.

Actually, in the middle of July, when Ludendorff was ready for his attack, he had a superiority in men by probably a quarter of a million, but he had overlooked in his calculation the value of tanks, and especially tanks co-operating with aeroplanes, of which we had a preponderance.

B

Another miscalculation was that the U-boats would stop the arrival of the American reinforcements which had been training in the United States for the past year. They were now urgently required owing to the Allies' heavy losses during the spring of 1918. The Americans had a great reservoir of man power, and, though they were short of transports and escorting vessels, the British Navy was able to supply two-thirds of their requirements in this respect, and with the help of the French to provide the necessary guns, tanks and aeroplanes for their support on the battlefield.

Tanks created surprise, economized man power and cleared a path for the infantry. These factors, combined with Foch's strategy of mobility for convergent attacks, were to be used fully until final victory had been won. Ludendorff's bludgeon methods were foiled and defeated by Foch's skill in planning, and by his surprise tactics.

The Battle of Cambrai in November, 1917, had proved that tactical surprise could be obtained by tanks, as the long bombardment, which had been a preliminary to the attack could be eliminated with the slow and costly preparation involved in an elaborate fire plan. Now it was to be conclusively proved that tanks starting the attack covered by a powerful artillery screen of shells could overrun the enemy machine guns and subjugate their riflemen, who could easily be dealt with by the following infantry. Such an operation took place on 4th July for the capture of the village of Hamel and to clear the Villers Bretonneux plateau with a view to freeing Amiens later. The Australian Corps, with sixty tanks, carried out this operation according to plan, and captured 1,500 prisoners without a single tankman being killed.

It was then apparent that an attack could be rapidly planned and carried out without elaborate preparations in any area where there were prospects of success.

Ludendorff, on the other hand, made no change at all in his plans, which were exactly similar to those made for the offensives undertaken on 21st March and 27th May.

On 15th July one German army was to cross the River Marne east of Château-Thierry, and two others, the First and Third, some thirty miles east of their Seventh Army at Château-Thierry, were to converge on a town twelve miles south of Reims, and then were to advance together a further twenty miles on Chalons. Ludendorff had so far made no call on the troops of Crown Prince Rupprecht's army group. It was indeed an ambitious plan against an enemy with a superiority in tanks and aeroplanes and in dealing with such a master of war as the Allied Generalissimo Foch.

Once again, too, there was no diversion or attempt to draw off the Allies' reserves by an attack farther north, where the Germans were in strength, and where they had a valuable prize, namely, the Channel ports, within artillery range. These attacks on the Marne and in Champagne had not only been foreseen, but special preparations had been made to meet them. Little can have been done on the part of the Germans to deceive the Allies for this cumbrous attack, and it was obvious that the German right flank, south-west of Soissons, was a most critical point.

Their crossing of the River Marne was duly effected; but without artillery support south of the river, this attack came to a standstill. Similarly, the great attack by the First and Third German Armies east of Amiens was halted by General Gouraud's skilful defence, and by the use of tactics which had been so successful on the Arras front on 28th March. The forward positions were only lightly held when the enemy bombardment started.

These positions were then evacuated, and when the force of the enemy barrage had subsided and their infantry left their cover for the attack, they were met by such heavy fire and consequent losses that they were unable to advance. Only at two points did the enemy breach the defences, and these gaps were quickly closed. This failure and the weakening of the twenty-five divisions specially trained for the operation to isolate Reims and capture the railway running through this city, crippled Ludendorff's main plan. General Gouraud had lost only the ground deliberately vacated during the enemy's bombardment and also a few prisoners.

By noon on 16th July Ludendorff gave orders for the suspension of the offensive by the First and Third Armies, and for organization of the defence. The First German Army east of Château-Thierry and Dormans made some progress, but owing to the fine fighting of the 3rd and 28th American Divisions south-east of Château-Thierry and by the resistance on the Mountain of Reims by General Berthelot's army, the Seventh German Army was not able to make a junction with the troops facing General Gouraud's army. The situation, therefore, was critical for the German troops, and especially for those south of the Marne. It was found to be impossible for their First Army to continue the offensive even with purely local attacks until after much preparation. Ludendorff then left this front, not completely realizing the danger of his position. He was apparently absorbed in the difficulty of his decision as to whether he should attempt to advance farther across the Marne or to leave troops on the southern bank, or how he could continue the offensive north of this river.

His G.H.Q. were pressing him to continue his advance in order to surround Reims. He still had a preponderance of troops on the Western Front by a quarter of a million, and in spite of heavy losses should have been able to organize a strong reserve when his attacks were checked. Instead, he urged the Crown Prince to build up reserves from the troops that could be disengaged from the local areas of operations; and he also warned him to strengthen his right wing. He then left this vital area to confer with the Crown Prince Rupprecht as to the possibility of the Fourth and Sixth Armies continuing the attacks, which had been suspended at the end of April, for the capture of the commanding heights round Poperinghe and for the high ground about Hazebrouck. At this time when the whole of his concentration was required at a vital battle, which he had planned for the capture of Paris, Ludendorff had thus taken himself a hundred miles away from the scene of action to consider another problem. No wonder, in computing the strength of the opposing forces, that it is permissible to add in Foch's value as being worth at least an army corps as compared with the opposing commander.

His series of attacks delivered in rapid succession and at different points, to mystify and mislead Ludendorff and make him direct his reserves to the wrong places, were far more effective than the heavy and ponderous blows delivered by Ludendorff after long pauses between each. The Allies were materially helped by the possession of more material than the Germans had. Ludendorff would have done better to try a series of withdrawals on our front, leaving the Allies the choice between hastily prepared battles to follow up the enemy, or, if they had refrained, there would have been the consequent loss of morale due to an admission of inability to take an offered opportunity for attack.

Foch, of course, as always, was on the spot where vital decisions had to be made. He was able to visualize the dangerous situations of the Germans in the salient, and to judge when the moment had arrived for a counter-attack with all available troops on the spot. By the time Ludendorff returned from his visit to the northern front on 17th July the position on the right of his Seventh Army had become serious. Much ground had been gained by the Allies between the River Ourcq and the River Aisne, and the division specially sent south-west of Soissons had given way.

A counter-stroke now had every prospect of success for Foch at the most unfavourable moment for the Germans, namely, in the course of an offensive, when they had been completely repulsed by the Fourth French Army and they were disordered by the failure of their attack.

The situation, however, for Foch on his intended front of attack of some twenty-five miles from the Aisne to beyond the Ourcy was not altogether easy.

He was determined to attack the whole of the German eastern flank with all available reserves; and these reserves were by no means fresh troops. However, on 18th July the French Tenth and Sixth Armies, with thirteen battalions of tanks, were able to assault the western flank of the Château-Thierry salient.

The French divisions had had long defensive struggles against the attacks of the Crown Prince's army, and the 1st and 2nd American Divisions had had much fighting in their long tours of duty in the line. However, full use was to be made of our superiority in tanks to gain the valuable advantage of surprise. Our method was to start with an intensive bombardment to drive the Germans from their forward positions and to cut their line communications. Then the tanks were to crash through the defences to make paths for infantry. In this way the French and American troops overran the lines of defence, so that by the evening of 19th July the guns of the Allies dominated the line of supply through Soissons. This was the channel of maintenance for the troops in the Marne salient.

So the situation which Ludendorff had to meet now on his return to this vital part of his front was that by Foch's counter-stroke much ground had been gained between the Ourcq and the Aisne; and that his troops south-west of Soissons had been forced to make considerable withdrawals. Although his troops south of the Ourcq were holding their ground, the position was precarious in view of the danger to their northern flank. Therefore, a general withdrawal had to be carried out on the western flank of the Soissons—Reims salient.

As the guns of the Allies were able to shell the railway north-east of Soissons it became increasingly difficult to bring up reinforcements to the most threatened and vitally important part of the salient, namely, its base.

A drive by the Allies in an easterly direction across this base would jeopardize the existence of all the troops in the front of the salient. However, infantry could now only be brought up to the battle area from some distance by lorry. This caused great delay in stemming the offensive. Also supply difficulties for ammunition and food increased. There were still troops south of the River Marne, so the Château-Thierry salient had to be held at all costs until the troops had been evacuated from the south bank. On 20th July eight German divisions recrossed the river under the concentrated fire of the French batteries from the high ground on their flanks. On the 21st the French and Americans by their advance in an easterly direction made the position at Château-Thierry untenable. On that evening the American 3rd Division was in this town.

The situation of the German army in the Marne salient was now grave not only on account of the danger to the flank but also because of its communications. Reinforcements would have to be detrained north of the River Aisne and would be tired on arrival at an ill-defined front. The morale of the troops in the salient was shaken by the prospect of further successes in the Soissons area in their rear. In consequence, on 22nd July an order was given for a withdrawal of troops on the southern front of the salient to a position some seven miles farther back parallel with the River Aisne on the night of 26th/27th July. Already 25,000 prisoners and 400 guns had been captured. The retreat by night on encumbered roads through broken country was a difficult and demoralizing operation, and it was very costly in life and material. That it was achieved at all in view of the pressure of the troops under Degoutte and de Mitry with five American divisions must be recorded as a creditable performance by the German troops.

On the following days the pressure of the Allies continued fiercely, and relief for the Germans by fresh divisions was continually necessary. But on 26th July, in spite of the success by our 26th Scottish Division east of the main Soissons—Château-Thierry road, and the advance of Degoutte's army, the German counter-attacks materialized with the divisions sent from Rupprecht's reserves.

It was the enemy's last and costly attempt to hold the Ourcq Valley. Two American divisions were largely instrumental by their fine fighting in breaking up their attacks. The First and Seventh German Armies were now losing heavily in men and material. At this time Mangin's army was slowly advancing up the hills east of the Soissons —Château-Thierry road. By 28th July, however, the key-point at Buzancy fell to the 15th Scottish Division, and the Germans were now badly shaken. More reinforcements were rushed down straight to the forward positions. It was obvious that leadership on the German side was slipping, and that Ludendorff was conforming to the will of the Allied Generalissimo. The German troops were resisting strongly in accordance with their orders, while Foch was determined to capture the hills that would overlook the downland to the Vesle, and so to turn their right flank on a line which they hoped to be able to hold.

On 1st August Mangin's Tenth Army, hidden in the forest of Villers Cotterêts, attacked. In spite of more reinforcements from Rupprecht's army being used up in abortive counter-attacks the first Allied objective was gained. The German front between the Ourcq and the Vesle had been turned, and the hold on Soissons was insecure. The enemy's resistance now weakened, and the Allied lines advanced. Soissons and some 40,000 prisoners were captured. The four French armies continued to press forward on the contracting German front. By 5th August the Aisne was crossed east of Soissons; and on the following day there was an advance on the northern banks of the Vesle. The Germans now made an effort to stand on the Aisne defences, but they still had to pay a heavy toll in stabilizing their line. Most of their gains since 27th May had been liquidated.

The Crown Prince had engaged seventy-four divisions, so that he had no local reserves left. Units were 30 per cent. below strength, and divisions were being decreased. Austrian divisions were being transported to France. At least ten divisions had been eliminated. This second Marne battle may be described as the turning point of the war.

Safety for Ludendorff now depended on his ability to build up a new reserve as soon as possible, as the initiative had definitely passed to the Allies, and the only means at his disposal was to shorten his front and straighten the existing salients at Montdidier and on the River Lys.

Foch was now in a position to carry out his plan of a series of offensive operations continued until the enemy's reserves were fully engaged. He would then attack in another convergent direction. Each of his convergent attacks was to have a direct bearing on the other. He had won the Second Battle of the Marne in this manner without a mass of manœuvre or superiority of man power. He had attacked no farther than the limit fixed by the advantage of surprise, and then he had struck elsewhere. Ludendorff throughout was expending his reserves to stop attacks or to try to retrieve situations with counter-strokes.

3.—PLAN AND OPERATIONS

The operations on the Marne had destroyed the last substantial reserves of the Germans and opened the way for our offensive farther north. On 23rd July Foch had disclosed his plan. It had been to liberate the northern coalmines, reduce the St. Mihiel salient and to free the Nancy and Paris—Amiens lines. He was, also, now preparing to carry out his continuous offensive operations on the whole front.

The operations were to start on Thursday, 8th August, by the III British Corps with a regiment of the 33rd American Division, the Australian and Canadian Corps of the Fourth British Army against Prince Rupprecht's forces south of the Somme, on a front of twelve miles prolonged to the south by the First French Army on a front of four miles.

There were to be 430 fighting tanks, including ninety-six of the new light Whippet type, with 150 in reserve for repair and supply services. No. 8 Squadron, R.A.F., was attached to the Tank Corps. The fire plan of the attack was to be carried out by 1,386 field guns and howitzers, twenty-six medium artillery brigades and thirteen heavy batteries. The assault was not to be preceded by bombardment or registration. The fire of the guns and howitzers was to precede the assault of the Australian, Canadian and III Corps. Surprise was to be the essence of Allied success. In local reserve were the Cavalry Corps and a division of the IX Corps. In general reserve were the French

Cavalry Corps. But Foch had seventy-seven other divisions on which he could call. Actually on the front of attack there was only a small margin of superiority of man power over the Germans, which consisted of Crown Prince Rupprecht's group of armies, the Second Army of ten divisions in forward positions and four in reserve. Their trenches were meagre and unconnected, poorly wired and with posts which were not mutually supporting. Their machine guns were numerous, concealed and posted in depth. After the continuously heavy fighting there was a deterioration in morale and discipline, and desertions were becoming numerous.

At 4.20 a.m. on 8th August the infantry, preceded by tanks and artillery bombardment, advanced north and south of the River Somme and by nightfall had overrun the enemy's positions to an average depth of seven miles. On the following days the advance was continued until by the 13th the British had penetrated to a depth of twelve miles. The Germans, then finding their position in the Montdidier salient too vulnerable, withdrew to a line from Bray through Roye to Noyon. Now further pressure was exerted by the Third Army on 21st August advancing north of the River Ancre and forcing the enemy back. On 22nd August Albert was captured and two days later Thiepval fell. The Third and Fourth Armies continued the offensive across the old Somme battlefield. By the 29th Combles and Bapaume were in our hands, and we were established on the left bank of the Somme. By a great feat of arms on the following night the Australians captured Mt. St. Quentin. Péronne then fell and the line of the Somme was dominated. The Third and Fourth Armies in the past ten days had captured more than 34,000 prisoners. The Germans were now compelled to abandon the Lys salient in order to economize man power, and it was becoming evident that their next line of resistance was to be the Hindenburg Line.

During these ten days pressure was being brought to bear on the First Army attacking on 26th August east of Arras on either side of the River Scarpe. By 2nd September Quéant was captured and the Germans began to withdraw from the line of the River Somme.

The enemy were now making an effort to hold the former trench systems west of the Hindenburg Line.

CHAPTER II

EVENTS LEADING UP TO THE BATTLE OF AMIENS, 8TH AUGUST, 1918

As has already been noted, the British and French armies had been improving their positions during July in spite of Ludendorff's attempt to march on Paris.

It was realized early in August that the German armies would have to stand on the defensive. It was expected that the Allies might attack in several directions, but the Amiens front was not specifically considered as a likely point for our advance. There were many alternatives for Foch. He might attack the St. Mihiel salient, the position east of Reims or on the Mt. Kemmel front. For the British Commander-in-Chief there were two possible lines of attack : namely, on the Lys or on the Somme.

The Germans, however, very soon ordered a withdrawal in the Lys Plain and from the Ancre and Avre bridgeheads.

On 6th August the 27th German Division attacked on the front planned for our attack on 8th August. This was somewhat disconcerting, as one division was changing its position, and on the front of the other division reliefs were taking place. The Germans were able to penetrate to a depth of 800 yards on a front of one and a half miles.

The situation was partially restored on the following morning, but considerable dislocation had occurred in adjusting plans for the 8th of August on that part of our front.

Much trouble had been taken to make the surprise as complete as possible. The Canadian First Army was not brought down from the north until the day before the battle.

The notice "Keep Your Mouth Shut" was pasted into every man's smallbook. The word "offensive" was never used.

Civilians left in Amiens were controlled by a chain of posts to check the entry of those without passes. Artillery fire was maintained with routine counter-battery and harassing work. All troop and transport movement took place by night. The R.A.F. were specially active in the Second Army area up to two days before the battle, and there was to be equal activity on the fronts of the First and Third Armies. Misleading daylight moves were carried out in other army areas.

The result was that the enemy had no exact idea where our reserves were to be employed. There was no suspicion that the Fourth Army was to blaze into activity behind a creeping barrage of guns and

13

howitzers in the thick mist, and that 523 aeroplanes were available to give their support.

An hour before sunrise on the morning of 8th August our air attacks had prevented the enemy from having any observation over our forward positions or communications.

The general course for the operations was for the enemy to be driven out of range of Amiens and the Paris railway, and their communications were to be interrupted by the occupation of a position twenty-five miles east of Amiens in the British front line of February, 1917. The Roman roads running east and south-east from Amiens made excellent advance lines for assaulting troops. Between the Somme and the Avre was open upland, which presented no natural obstacle to tanks. The ground was soaked with rain and mist during the first week in August.

The details of the plan for this battle were for an advance to be carried out as rapidly as possible to the old Amiens defence line after zero hour at 4.20 a.m. approximately seven miles from the starting line at its farthest point. On reaching this line there was to be consolidation, and then exploitation up to the old British front line. The Cavalry Corps was to be prepared to pass through anywhere south of the Somme and the Roman road running south-east from Amiens. The role of the First French Army on our right was to maintain contact with the XXI Corps nearest to the Canadian Corps, starting forty-five minutes after zero. Two battalions of light tanks were allotted to this corps. The IX Corps, south of it, was to start three and a quarter hours later and advance two miles into the enemy's position to protect the right flank of the French corps on its left. The next French corps, the X, was to cover the right of the corps on its left, and their other corps was to prepare to attack farther south. The Army Commander, however, added that the attacks were to be conducted in order to achieve the greatest rapidity in a succession of forward bounds.

It is apparent that the lack of heavy tanks and the late hour of starting were a handicap from which it was difficult to recover when the effect of surprise had passed after the initial attack by our Fourth Army.

CHAPTER III

THE FIRST DAY OF THE BATTLE OF AMIENS

CONSIDERED FROM THE POINT OF VIEW OF THE APPLICATION OF THE PRINCIPLES OF WAR

1. Surprise is a most powerful weapon. By means of surprise it is possible to create situations for which the enemy is unprepared, and so to upset him and force him either to unconsidered action or to complete inaction. Its value, however, must be proportional to the time taken by the enemy to recover and to take retaliatory measures. In this case it was gained by secrecy, by calculated deception and stratagem in moving the Canadian Corps into position as late as possible for the assault at 4.20 a.m. on 8th August, and by the unexpected rapidity of movement of 430 tanks in an unsuspected direction east of Amiens.

In this case the use of our greatly improved weapon, the tank, had not been prematurely disclosed, and on our front they were in ample quantity. A warning with reference to the full use of our powerful weapon, namely, surprise, must be that it cannot be continuously maintained. Much of its effect may be lost if there are insufficient reserves for exploitation.

As a result of our complete preliminary arrangements for surprise no enemy counter-preparations on 7th August unduly interfered with the arrangements of our Canadian and Australian forces and the First French Army for the dawn and subsequent attacks on the following day. There were intermittent gas and H.E. bombardments only. This was a remarkable achievement, because the opposing sides were between three and five hundred yards apart.

So complete was the surprise that when the fire plan started, and the infantry advanced, it was more than five minutes before the enemy replied by fire on to our assembly positions, which had by that time been vacated.

In the centre there was a continuous success, as the Canadians and Australians advanced steadily. By 11 a.m. they were in the Amiens defence line, having fought their way forward, at the farthest place, for three miles from their starting point. The tanks had materially helped in overcoming strong-points and in assisting the advance with their fire. By the speed of their advance they had captured a divisional staff, and taken prisoners in billets in German villages, including a party of officers having breakfast in their mess.

15

By this first nightfall eight miles of the Amiens defence line, nine miles at its farthest point from our original positions, except for a mile above the Roman road, had been captured.

There was, however, now a distinct salient on our front, as the corps on either side of the Australians and Canadians had not been able to come into line. On the northern flank the country was enclosed, and there were strong-points, from which the enemy counter-attacked with success; and on the four miles of front on the southern side the French had difficulties in the woods and villages. However, the success of this day's fighting may be summed up as being due to brilliant tactical surprise, the efficiency of the tanks, the co-operation and mobility of the cavalry advancing in some parts over twenty miles from their assembly areas, and to the work of the R.E., whose undemonstrative operations, as always, cleared the way for the advance, removed obstacles and greatly facilitated every task of the assaulting troops. No task is ever too difficult for them. It may be said for the Royal Engineers that all obstacles will be overcome in time; miracles take longer. So unobtrusively and skilfully are all demands on their efficiency met, that they are taken for granted in the general co-operation.

But this first day of fighting in the open added even to the variety of their many and difficult duties. We read with admiration that when a heavy railway gun was noticed in no-man's-land the Engineers went out, shunted the train, and drove it with the gun inside our lines. Just another of their great feats of this day of victory, to which they contributed in such very full measure. The support of the artillery was so close and effective, not only in the initial phases but in the capture of woods, villages and other centres of resistance throughout the day, that they added even to their own marvellous record throughout the battles of this war. They gave the timely and accurate help that was required throughout the whole day's fighting to enable the impetus of the assault to be maintained. The Royal Corps of Signals, as usual, had to contend with the great difficulties of interrupted communications, of units being diverted from arranged centres of advance and of the whole front being indistinguishable between our own and the enemy troops. That they effected marvels in helping to maintain contact, and to enable commanders to keep in touch with scattered units, is a faint indication of their untiring efforts, their skill and courage and their self-sacrifice.

It had indeed been a day of general co-operation, although results had been unequal.

The victory on this day exemplified the principle that offensive action confers great advantages. The Canadian Corps not only gained the Amiens defence line on nearly the whole front between the two

Roman roads, some fifty square miles, but they captured over 5,000 prisoners and 161 guns and many hundreds of machine guns. The Australian Corps operating between the Somme and the Roman road occupied approximately thirty square miles of country on reaching the line held by the Canadian Corps, and they captured nearly 8,000 prisoners and 173 guns.

On the left of the Australian Corps the III Corps between the Somme and the Ancre had many more difficulties to contend with than on the other fronts. There were three strong enemy divisions here and an attack had been made by their 27th Division against the centre of the front on 6th August, and trenches had been lost, so that re-adjustment had to be made for assembly positions and starting lines as well as fire-plan alterations for zero hour on 8th August. Also, enemy gas shells had caused casualties during the night of 7th/8th August during relief of the forward trenches. The enemy, too, were alert at zero hour, as they were expecting a counter-attack for the recapture of the ground they had gained on 6th August. In addition, on this flank there were no cavalry and there was only one tank battalion.

The strongly fortified villages and woods in the area on the front of the III Corps against an enemy practically equal in strength made progress difficult in spite of the close and effective support of the artillery. Intercommunication and co-operation across their boundary, the River Somme, with the Australians on their flank were a constant difficulty. On the following day this inter-corps boundary was changed. The Australians included the River Somme in their area of advance, with the boundary along a road about half a mile north of the river and parallel to it. By the end of this day the main attack of the III Corps was short of the front held by the Canadians and Australians. They had been checked on the first objective; but they captured some 600 prisoners.

The co-operation of the army and the air force was fully exemplified not only in the early assault with the tanks but with their contact aeroplanes throughout the morning. They materially assisted with information both to commanders and to artillery, and also later with the bombing of the Somme bridges with over 200 flights at a cost of 13 per cent. of their day flying strength. The French army on the right flank were not able to catch up the Canadian Corps on their left flank owing to their later start, but they captured over 3,300 prisoners and nearly 300 guns.

The results of the day's fighting justified the orders for the renewal of the offensive on 9th August. The absence of complete success on our flanks did not detract from the victories of the two corps in our centre in spite of our losses of 25 per cent. of the tanks engaged. Our principle of war that offensive action should be undertaken wherever the circumstances are favourable was thus exemplified. The objective for the day had been wisely chosen within the means available. It had been possible to concentrate the bulk of our resources for the attainment of that objective. By skilful economy of force and distribution of the arms it had been possible to gain a firm foundation against counter-attack on the front of the two centre corps at the Amiens defences on which to base further offensive action for 9th August to the British front line of February, 1917, some seven miles farther east. In pursuance of these principles of war there was every prospect of success against the enemy's organized positions from the River Aisne, east of Soissons, continuing in a northerly direction; especially as the enemy admitted that six or seven battleworthy divisions had been completely broken, and that only three or four others were available to close the broad gaps on their front and to oppose further resistance. The enemy reports, also, showed that they considered that our losses had been proportionately small, and that the numerical balance was swinging against them, and that as more American troops arrived it would be increasingly unfavourable. Counter-attack with their dwindling reserves was impossible on a large scale.

Ludendorff now reported that his war machine was no longer efficient, and that his fighting power had suffered, even though the great majority of divisions fought heroically. But, he added, the 8th of August put the decline of that fighting power beyond all doubt, and in such a situation he thought that he had no hope of finding a strategic expedient whereby to turn the situation to his advantage. On the contrary, he became convinced that the Army was now without a safe basis for the plans of G.H.Q., on which he had hitherto been able to build. The 8th of August, he said, opened the eyes of the staff on both sides, and as soon as he had grasped the whole situation brought about by the events on this day he decided to arrange conferences with the Imperial Chancellor and the Secretary of State for Foreign Affairs in order to discuss peace questions.

CHAPTER IV

THE BATTLE OF AMIENS FROM 9TH AUGUST, 1918

THE Fourth Army operation orders for 9th August indicated a general advance on the whole front. The III Corps were to consolidate a strong position as a defensive flank to the Fourth Army. The main advance was to be made by the Canadian Corps, with the French on the right and the Australians on the left to cover their flanks. The orders given to the cavalry by its Corps Commander were to support the infantry of the Canadian Corps with the Whippet tanks attached to them. This was a most important day for the continuance of offensive operations before the enemy could be reinforced and re-established in freshly formed defences. However, there were now great difficulties in communication due to the change to open warfare after the years of trench warfare, and there were frequent breakdowns. Up to this time orders for separate units and formations hinged so much on mutual co-operation and co-ordination that intercommunication was vitally important. Limiting lines of advance until troops had arrived up to the same alignment to protect the flanks had always been the routine. But against a tired and defeated enemy justifiable risks may be taken. For instance, in the orders for this day the Canadian Corps were to advance between the Amiens—Roye road and the Amiens—Nesle railway and establish themselves on a general line Roye—Hallu.

The Australian Corps were to conform to the advance of the Canadian Corps and then establish themselves on a general line Lihons—Mericourt. When the III Corps were on a line running through Demarcourt, the Australians were to advance their left flank. All plans were carefully dovetailed into a completely co-ordinated plan on the whole front, depending for the most part on the Canadian Corps, who were to choose their time of start and inform others. So all depended on vital intercommunication, which in open country is much more difficult to maintain than in trench warfare.

Actually, the time was coming when, with a weakened enemy in the front no longer able to counter-attack on a large scale, but able if given time to patch up positions with reinforcements hastily brought up from a distance, it should be possible for divisions to operate independently towards distant objectives. It should be possible now to reinforce success only, and so by continuous pressure enable the whole advance to be continued, as enemy resistance and strong-points

19

would be engulfed by victorious troops on either side of them. This day, however, was only the second day of open warfare, so that it was not possible so quickly to conform to altered conditions for a change of ideas and of tactics.

The result was that, though substantial progress was made on 9th August, we were short of our objectives owing to delays in receipt of orders in the field, and there was lack of co-ordination in the advance owing to the uncertainty about the zero hour. It was unfortunate at this juncture that the offensive was not pressed throughout the whole front, as the two corps in the centre were soon through the enemy's main defences, and the six German reserve divisions brought into the line from considerable distances would be tired after train or long motor journeys and night marches, and would have difficulty in realizing the situation to co-operate with flank formations. In addition, these divisions arrived without directing staff, means of intercommunication or supporting artillery. They had to be sent into battle positions on arrival. Thus a strong co-operative movement on our whole front might on this day have given very considerable results. On the French front the corps on the right of the Canadian Corps had not been able to start until 8 a.m., but then an advance had been made of some two and a half miles, and, though they were checked by a fresh German division during the afternoon, they were able to join up in line with the right of the Canadian Corps under cover of darkness. The French had now captured nearly 4,500 prisoners and more than a hundred guns.

Ludendorff's report on the situation was that his Second Army was thoroughly disorganized, and that its losses had been very heavy. Great demands had been made on reserves to fill up the gaps.

Infantry had been going into action straight off their lorries while their artillery had been sent to another part of the line. Units were badly mixed up. The losses in prisoners had been so heavy that G.H.Q. was again faced with the necessity of breaking up divisions to form reserves. As there was no hope of materially improving his position by counter-attacks he considered that the only course was to hold on.

Actually, on 10th August the German resistance stiffened, and our offensive on the whole front was reduced. The British Commander-in-Chief now started to complete the details of his plans for the capture of La Bassée and the Aubers Ridge by the First Army in conjunction with an advance by the Third Army against Bapaume and by the Second Army against Mt. Kemmel.

Marshal Foch, however, wanted a further effort to be made, namely, for our Fourth Army to reach the Somme below Ham in order to prepare for a crossing, and at the same time to continue its action astride that river to reach Péronne. The French First Army were to support this advance.

The French Third Army were to exploit the advance of the French First Army and to clear the Montdidier area.

On this date the French Intelligence Service appreciated the situation to the effect that the enemy would now probably retire by bounds to shorten their front by approximately ninety miles, through the Siegfried positions, and the Hagen positions back to the Metz—Antwerp railway.

In the meantime, in accordance with the wishes and instructions of the Allied Generalissimo, orders were issued for the Fourth Army to press on to the Somme between Ham and Péronne, with the First Army advancing on the right. The III Corps on the left were to establish a defensive flank. However, now the Germans were increasing their resistance, and they had fresh troops with supporting artillery on our front. In addition, they had strong defensive positions in their area on the western edge of the ground cut up by the fighting in 1916, by the retreat to the Hindenburg Line in 1917, when they had thrown General Nivelle's plan out of gear; and also by the operations starting on 21st March of this year. Already crews and tanks had suffered heavily, and it was difficult to replace ammunition expended. Our twelve divisions and three cavalry divisions had been fighting since 4.20 a.m. on 8th August against an enemy who had thirty-five divisions, of which some twenty-two German divisions were still in action. Now the country was becoming increasingly difficult for the movement of cavalry and tanks and for artillery support to the advancing infantry. Under these conditions it was necessary to reconsider the situation on this front owing to the very considerable obstacles to a co-ordinated advance on a wide front with the co-operation of all arms. After deliberation with the Commander-in-Chief it was decided now to strike from the Albert—Arras front through Bapaume, and so to dislocate Ludendorff's plans for retreat by forcing the Germans from the Somme heights and by turning the line of the river from Péronne southwards. Ludendorff hoped to repeat the 1917 manoeuvres of a slow retirement, with our following troops in difficulties from the state of the country and the necessity to continue to attack strong defensive positions frontally. By attacking the northern edge of the base of the enemy's salient towards Amiens the costly frontal advance would be obviated, and the enemy's retirement would be accelerated by our pressure from an unexpected direction. The Generalissimo agreed to the discontinuance of the Amiens battle, as he recognized that the increased opposition in country suited for defensive operations had changed the situation. He asked that the proposed offensive operations by the Third Army might be under-

C

taken as soon as possible, while simultaneously the southern base of the Amiens salient was attacked by the French Tenth Army east of the River Oise.

The results of this Amiens battle may be summarized as follows. The enemy, by use of waning reserves, had fully utilized their old battle area, with its opportunities for defence, to gain a temporary cessation of the offensive on this front.

The complete results expected from this battle were not obtained, although nearly 30,000 prisoners and 500 guns were captured.

The German Eighteenth Army was able to withdraw on our right flank, although it had been outflanked by the advance of the Canadian Corps.

It was difficult for the staff of all formations to assimilate the new tactics required after the complete break-through on 8th August. A rapid appreciation of changed conditions obviously could not be easy after the years of stereotyped warfare, especially as intercommunication was so constantly interrupted by damage to wires and cables, and up and down routes for traffic had not been quickly organized.

There were isolated actions by small bodies of cavalry, which led to good results; but for the most part their use as a mounted arm in direct attack brought little advantage .

The losses in our tanks increased daily, until on the 10th we lost 50 per cent. of the numbers engaged.

The halt on the Amiens defence line captured on the afternoon of 8th August enabled the enemy to bring up thirteen reinforcing divisions during the next three days. Had it been possible for us to send fresh divisions on 9th August through those that had been fighting on the opening day of the battle, great results might have been obtained, and we might have been able to break through the old British front-line trenches of 1917 before the enemy could hold up our advance with divisions rushed up to fill gaps. The late starts made by the Canadian and Australian Corps on 9th August militated against our final success on this front when time was vitally important for us to exploit success as early as possible while the enemy on our immediate front was dispirited and disorganized.

As soon as the enemy was able to reorganize his defences, the infantry attacks, even with tanks, became increasingly costly.

Ludendorff, however, had now lost his hope of a counter-stroke on a large scale. He had only sixteen fresh divisions in reserve in the West.

He might expect to hold the line from Arras to the Oise until he could retreat to the Hindenburg Line for his winter quarters.

The Generalissimo, however, had no intention of allowing the Germans to make a retreat in their own time. He decided to strike as early as possible before Boehn, the newly appointed Army Group Commander of the Second, Eighteenth and Ninth Armies, could settle down in positions from Albert to Soissons between the armies of Prince Rupprecht and the German Crown Prince. On 17th August Mangin, commanding the French Tenth Army, attacked between the Oise and the Aisne against the German Ninth Army on a front of ten miles.

He was able to advance to a depth of approximately one mile and to capture nearly 2,000 prisoners. On the following days he extended his front of attack, advancing in the course of the next three days on to the western parts of the heights of the Aisne, having by 20th August captured 8,000 prisoners and 200 guns.

He was then in a position to threaten the enemy's line west of the River Oise.

Boehn was now forced to use some of his reserves for this operation. Ludendorff then became engaged on the front between the Avre and the Vesle. Foch, now having drawn some of the reserves away from their possible use on the northern flank of the Amiens salient, stopped Mangin's offensive operations on the night of the 20th. On the morning of Wednesday, 21st August, the British Third Army started their attack to turn from the north the line of the Somme towards the objective Cambrai—St. Quentin.

By a limited advance the Arras—Albert railway would be recovered, and then later an attack could be delivered north of the Somme by the Third and Fourth Armies.

CHAPTER V

OPERATIONS FROM 21st AUGUST, 1918

BEFORE the end of the Battle of Amiens, Ludendorff had tendered his resignation. He had endeavoured to encourage his forces with false hopes of impending victory and entry into Paris; instead he was forced to shorten his front on the Ancre and on the Lys, where we regained Lacon and Calonne. He was hoping to create a reserve. The reaction on the morale of the German Army and its leaders was inevitable.

Superior numbers of the enemy had been defeated in the Battle of Amiens, and over 20,000 prisoners had been captured. Since that date they had lost some 8,000 prisoners and 200 guns. Also much ground on the western part of the heights of the Aisne had been occupied by the French.

Foch was now arranging for a new battleground. The ground north of the Ancre was suitable for tanks, and the Siegfried Line was nearer his front between Arras and Albert. Therefore, Foch decided to strike on 21st August against the northern flank of the Germans' awkward salient in order to recover the Arras—Albert railway.

This action started by the Third Army was, however, to be part of a large co-ordinated operation with the Fourth Army covering the right flank and the First Army on the left ready to exploit success. The Second Army was to co-operate by containing the enemy on its front in an advance on Mt. Kemmel.

The Third Army advanced at 4.55 a.m. on 21st August in a thick fog. The result of this was that there was great difficulty for the attacking troops in keeping direction, especially as there was a smoke barrage as well. Artillery and machine-gun support could not be maintained, and many tanks could not gain contact. The advance, however, proceeded steadily on the front of the VI Corps, where the main line of German resistance, with some 1,200 prisoners, was captured by midday. This was the second objective. Similarly, on the front of the other two corps the advance by the infantry had been considerable. But exploitation by tanks and cavalry was not possible, for the enemy held strong positions, and there were at least eleven divisions on the front of the two armies.

It was expected that the Fourth Army would be able to occupy Albert on 22nd August to enable both armies to continue the offensive together on the 23rd.

On 22nd August, in the Third Army, preparations were made for a continuance of the advance, while the Fourth Army on their right eliminated the salient between the Somme and the Ancre, and the

18th Division recaptured Albert. The German counter-attacks against the Third Army north and south of the Ancre were successfully repulsed.

Boehn's Army Group was retiring to the south bank of the River Oise on this day between Guny and Pontoise.

On the 22nd the ground was now prepared for the continuance of a vigorous offensive by the Third Army with the co-operation of the Fourth Army in accordance with Foch's plan of operations for the extension of general pressure from the Scarpe to Soissons.

Accordingly, on 23rd August the general offensive usually called the Battle of Albert was undertaken by the Fourth and Third Armies and by the French Tenth Army. The Fourth Army gained ground on both banks of the River Somme to a depth of two miles on a front of four miles. The Third Army farther north was able to drive the enemy from the main line of resistance on the Arras—Albert railway. The R.A.F. was particularly active with low-flying attacks and with artillery co-operation on this day.

On the 24th the offensive was continued by the Fourth and Third Armies for the most part against scattered enemy machine guns, well sited in concealed positions ahead of the German main lines. These positions had to be specially dealt with by stalking parties covered by artillery, mortars and machine-gun fire.

On the following day the orders were for the First Army to be ready to co-operate with the Third Army and to attack the enemy south of the River Scarpe. It was foreseen that considerable strategic results might be obtained in future by the employment of the Cavalry Corps under its commander. Orders were given that detachments from it were not to be made except to corps and divisions, so that favourable situations might be exploited fully and readily. Satisfactory progress was made on the 25th. The enemy north of the River Somme fell back three miles, but on the Hindenburg Line the enemy held on to their positions, so that it was evident that further preparations would be necessary before an attack could be made in this area. South of the River Somme preparations were made for a further advance.

By the 26th we had been able to capture Avesnes, Le Sars and Martinpuich, but Bapaume was stubbornly defended.

The French were making progress in touch with one another and with the Fourth Army.

The French First Army captured important villages north and south-west of Roye after lively fighting.

The scene now changes for the main battle to the Scarpe for the First and Third Armies. As a result of the Battle of Albert the German General Staff admitted that their position between the Somme and the Oise was not secure, and that the army groups under Prince Rupprecht and under Boehn must now be withdrawn.

CHAPTER VI

THE BATTLE OF THE SCARPE

ORDERS had been issued on 15th August for preparations to be made for an advance by the First Army in an easterly direction from Arras between the left of the Third Army and the River Scarpe on a five-mile front. Locally the enemy were to be contained on the front of the First Army while the First and Fourth Armies were fighting farther south in the Battle of Albert.

Ludendorff was planning to withdraw Boehn's Army Group to the left bank of the Somme in front of Péronne and the canal between Ham and Noyon to cover their Siegfried system, which was now being reconstructed. Boehn, it was reported, was anxious to retain his position on the left bank of the Somme in front of Péronne as a pivot from which to outflank the area north of it as opportunity occurred. He had not realized that Field-Marshal Haig's counter-plans included an extension of the offensive northwards as far as the Scarpe, to enable his force to take the Siegfried positions in reverse after the capture of the Wotan Line farther north.

On 24th August orders had been given for the co-operation of the First Army on the left of the Third Army.

The First Army was to endeavour, after capturing the Drocourt-Quéant Line close to its boundary with the Third Army, to operate against the right flank of the enemy in front of the Third Army.

For this general offensive the Commander-in-Chief emphasized the changed conditions, and the necessity to meet them with a new technique. It was now necessary to get rid of the ideas and methods of command to which all had become accustomed during the past years. It was now important for all units to use increased initiative, and to act with the greatest possible boldness and resolution to gain the fullest advantage against an enemy who had been continuously attacked for the past month and had had two severe defeats. Unit commanders of all ranks were urged to keep in mind the need to assist their neighbours to press on. Limited objectives were not necessary against an enemy no longer able to organize heavy counter-attacks with all arms or to hold a front strongly at all points on such an extended front of attack, namely, 120 miles from Reims to the River Scarpe.

The Commander-in-Chief directed in future that divisions should be given distant objectives to be reached independently even if the flanks were exposed temporarily.

Success was to be reinforced. Vigorous offensive was to be continued where the enemy was weak. Such procedure would cause hostile strong-points to fall. The final recommendation was for all to act energetically and without hesitation, and to push forward to the objective.

In addition, staff duties would undoubtedly increase. Liaison officers at the front would be required to assist with the latest information for units about the situation on the flanks and to be in touch with their superiors to pass back news and to obtain support where and when it was required. Such transitions from stereotyped conditions to open warfare were not easy to accomplish suddenly. But as the results that were subsequently attained were the prelude to victory it shows that there was loyal effort on the part of all to co-operate in the great convergent attacks.

That the extension of the Allied offensive was a very great success was evident even by the evening of 26th August, when the German Seventeenth, Second and Eighteenth Armies were starting their involuntary withdrawal to cover the Hindenburg Line on a general line east of Noyon to positions opposite Arras pivoting on the Wotan position. For the next three days the Germans continued their retreat. Every day they lost many prisoners and much material. Also, their bold use of field guns, machine guns and mortars in covering their rearward infantry caused them considerable losses in these weapons.

By Thursday, 29th August, Boehn's Army Group was still fighting for time to get back to its support lines, and at the same time orders were issued for the preparation of new positions from the River Scheldt to the River Meuse in the Hermann, Hagen and Freya Lines.

On this day the loss of Bapaume to the New Zealanders was a grave blow to the Germans, for they were now driven from the Somme Plateau, and they not only lost large quantities of stores but the road to Cambrai was open to the Third Army. Another important point that had fallen to us on this day was Greenland Hill to the First Army in the north. South of the River Somme we had occupied Ham and the western bank opposite Péronne. The French First Army was on our right along this river, and Humbert occupied Noyon. On the 30th above the southern boundary of the First and Third Armies there was an important advance on a front of three miles towards the Drocourt-Quéant Switch.

Farther south the Third Army entered Bullecourt and was advancing towards Vaulx Wood, some five miles south of it. In the early hours of 31st August the 5th Australian Brigade, who had previously under cover of darkness crossed the River Somme, and by another dashing exploit captured the enemy trenches south-east of Cléry, rushed Mt. St. Quentin, dominating Péronne.

This was strongly held by picked troops. The attack was made with the minimum of artillery support in order to gain the advantage of surprise. As a result of this very gallant achievement, the Australians entered Péronne. Thus the Somme defences for some twenty miles as far south as Ham were turned.

The operations of the 2nd Australian Division from 27th August to 2nd September, 1918, during which period they advanced from Cappy to the outskirts of Péronne, forced the passage of the Somme and captured Mt. St. Quentin, are so outstanding that they deserve our close examination as to the cause of their great successes. It is important to note the part played by the rifle grenade during this fighting and to realize that tactical successes were often due to this valuable weapon.

After midnight on 26th/27th August the 2nd Australian Division started to advance from the vicinity of Cappy to the Somme on an average frontage of 6,000 yards. On 30th August the 5th Brigade crossed the Somme at Feuilleres and cleared the village of Cléry-sur-Somme in an advance of 4,000 yards. On 31st August this brigade attacked the high ground of Mt. St. Quentin, advancing about 2,000 yards on a similar frontage. They gained a footing in the village, but counter-attacks dislodged them. On 1st September the 6th Brigade passed through the 5th Brigade, captured Mt. St. Quentin and held it to a depth of 1,500 yards. On 2nd September the 7th Brigade advanced through the 6th Brigade and cleared the village of Haut-Allaine, adjoining the eastern side of Mt. St. Quentin, to a depth of 2,500 yards on a frontage of 2,000 yards. By 4th September the Division had captured 15,000 acres, including fourteen villages. It had captured over 1,600 prisoners, two field guns, 265 machine guns and eighteen trench mortars. It had inflicted heavy losses on the enemy in killed and wounded. Mt. St. Quentin was the key to Péronne. Its capture led directly to the evacuation by the enemy of all the territory eastward back to the Hindenburg Line.

The operations of the 5th Brigade during the first four days of this operation were most noteworthy. This brigade fought continuously for four days, made a magnificent advance of over 8,000 yards, then crossed the Somme and captured trenches against strong opposition. Finally they stormed the village of Mt. St. Quentin, which had a strong trench system on a dominant height with a long field of fire.

The fighting which took place was not the usual trench-warfare type. The attacks were ordered at such short notice that it had not been found practicable to employ a creeping barrage. During the advance to the Somme, artillery brigades working with battalion commanders moved forward by batteries. In certain special cases, sections were detailed to work in close touch with company commanders for short periods. The artillery support to the infantry was invaluable, and information of many points of resistance was obtained first hand by batteries, which engaged these strong-points at once with very satisfactory results. For the attacks on Mt. St. Quentin on 31st August and 1st September it was found necessary to group the field artillery brigades so that concentrations on a timed programme could be arranged on selected localities. The fire was adjusted and maintained according to the rate of the infantry progress. The heavy artillery was similarly used, its fire being placed on the same areas with earlier lifts.

Machine-gun support was afforded by the 2nd Australian Machine Gun Battalion. The brigade commanders allotted sections of machine guns to work with each attacking battalion during the advance; any remaining guns being pushed forward later to cover gaps. On many occasions it was possible to disperse large parties of the enemy by direct fire. On the morning of 2nd September about 500 of the enemy were engaged at a range of 2,200 yards, in spite of the fact that very long distances had to be covered by man-handling, owing to the enemy's advantages in observation facilities, both naturally and by balloon.

The main fighting took place in the Somme Valley to the west of Péronne and on the high ground of Mt. St. Quentin north of Péronne. Mt. St. Quentin was the key of the whole German position east of the Somme. The fall of Péronne was certain on the capture of this height. It was therefore most stubbornly defended. The ground rises steeply on the north, west and south sides, and the ruins of the village were just below its western side. The ground offered every opportunity for prolonged defence, being covered with a maze of old trenches, wire and shell-holes, relics of the desperate fighting which took place there in 1916. Also there was plenty of natural cover for the defenders. From prisoners' statements it was learnt that the German Command had issued instructions that the position was to be held at all costs, and that the garrison had specially trained troops. The garrison fought hard to carry out these orders.

The German system of defence was in depth, with the machine gun as the backbone of the defence. There were forward defended localities covered by the cross-fire of artillery as well as machine-gun fire.

On this account and owing to the system of defending their ground employed by the Germans, the fighting which took place during the whole of these operations was never at all static. Actually, fighting conditions approximated to those of open warfare. But in spite of strong machine-gun defence the infantry did advance rapidly and deeply into the enemy's position; as the morale of the enemy's infantry in 1918 had deteriorated from its earlier standard. This could not be said of the German machine gunners, who were still skilful and brave fighters, but our infantry continued to advance on occasions when time did not permit of arranging for the close support of artillery. This was due, it had been reported, to the effective technique evolved by the close co-operation of rifle, light machine gun and grenade.

When conditions as to range and cover were suitable the Lewis guns took positions from which they could open fire on the objective, and the rifle and grenade sections selected the best-covered line of approach to the objective, and reached effective range.

Constantly by these means of close co-operation of company weapons, the 2nd Australian Division infantry penetrated the machine-gun defences of the Germans at Mt. St. Quentin. Many posts were captured by the high-angle grenade fire and with the fire of Lewis guns. The results of the fighting were that 265 machine guns were captured in seven days' fighting.

The success of many of the attacks was dependent upon platoon weapons in the final assault. That Péronne eventually fell after the capture of Mt. St. Quentin was due to the very highest standard of training in the Australian infantry, who were able to use their weapons to the very best advantage to supplement at every stage their supporting fire. They had by their training overcome the difficulty of maintaining co-ordination between the assaulting infantry and the artillery, mortars and machine guns, so that when necessary their own fire was adequate to enable them to overcome the most stubborn resistance of the defenders of commanding positions.

In the battles of these last six days thirty-five German divisions had been driven back over the country, which had been the battleground of the River Somme fighting in 1916, and they had lost 34,000 prisoners and 270 guns.

Ludendorff's retreat was rapidly reducing his reserves instead of, as he had hoped, economizing his resources.

By the morning of 2nd September the First Army were in position to attack the northern extension of the Hindenburg Line, connected at Quéant to the Drocourt-Quéant Switch. Much work had been carried out on this position during the past eighteen months. It was the key of the whole German front, and they held it with eleven divisions up to the Sensée River. It was assaulted by two Canadian and four British divisions with forty tanks. On their actual front of attack they had nine German divisions holding very strong positions in depth, which they considered were impregnable. Yet, in seven hours, the attackers forced through all the lines of this strongest position in the West on a front of six miles with the capture of 8,000 prisoners. With their right flank threatened, the Germans south of Quéant had to hurry back.

Ludendorff's plan for an immediate withdrawal was now impossible, nor could he organize counter-attacks. He had to hurry his troops behind the Canal du Nord and rely temporarily on the obstacles of the marshes in the Sensée Valley west of Douai and the Agache River. By 4th September the pursuing divisions of the First Army were on the canal bank, where they found the enemy entrenched on the eastern bank.

On this day the Fourth Army was pressing on east of Péronne and the Third Army was three miles east of Bapaume and through Bullecourt, six miles to the north. On the following day both the Fourth and First French Armies had crossed the River Somme. Mangin's army was moving eastwards along the Chemin des Dames. In Flanders we had recovered Neuve Chapelle and Fauquis; and north of the River Lys our front was from Voormezeele to Ploegsteert. Lens had been evacuated. There was no hope for the Germans to make an intermediate stand before the Siegfried zone.

For a few days now the Allies were occupied only in maintaining pressure on the German retreat. The immediate plan was to prepare for the final battle, for which Foch had been planning since July.

Douai was covered by a line of water obstacles; Cambrai and St. Quentin by the Siegfried positions; and Laon by the difficult country between the St. Gobain Forest, the Oise and the Aislette Valley.

The German *communiqué* reported that we had not succeeded in breaking through anywhere between Soissons and Arras.

The reason was that whenever we had gained a success they had twice withdrawn on a large front. The prospects of exploiting an immediate break-through on the front were doubtful, as the Germans still had reserves. Since 8th August they had been forced to withdraw along the whole of our front, that is, up to fourteen miles on the front of the Fourth Army, fifteen miles on the front of the Third Army, and twelve miles on the front of the First Army. Up to 3rd September, 108,771 prisoners had been captured on our front.

It was necessary now to rest the troops, to conserve resources and to improve communications in order to prepare for the final vigorous offensive, which was to be carried out by the Allies on the whole front.

Between 12th and 18th September the enemy were driven from the former British trench system west of the Hindenburg Line. They were back again in the positions to which they had withdrawn in the spring of 1917.

This time their reserves and resources were depleted, and their army was on the point of being finally defeated.

CHAPTER VII

QUESTIONS

1. What was the effect of the great successes gained during the battles of the Hindenburg Line?

2. Give instances of the use of railways.

3. Describe the fighting from 18th September to 4th November, 1918.

4. Describe the fighting from 2nd to 5th November, 1918, towards the line Maubeuge—Mons.

5. Describe the series of operations from 7th October, 1918, to the end of the month towards Le Quesnoy and Valenciennes.

6. Describe the battle of 8th August, 1918.

7. Discuss the plans made on 20th September, 1918. What was the result by 17th October, 1918?

8. Give instances of the use of tanks from 8th August to 17th October, 1918.

9. (a) Discuss the use of reserves in this campaign; and
   (b) Discuss the effect of the four convergent attacks starting on 22nd September, 1918.

10. How did supplies affect the situation after 8th March, 1918?

11. What were the plans and operations for the River Scarpe battle?

12. Illustrate the principles of war.

GENERAL NOTES FOR SOLUTION
OF QUESTIONS

By the middle of August, 1918, the Germans between the Somme and the Oise were almost everywhere back in their 1916 positions. Then, in accordance with the idea of confining the attacks to limited objectives, this attack was stopped.

The Amiens salient, like the Marne salient, had been eliminated. The main lines of railway through Amiens, which the enemy had dominated since the end of March, and which were the main channels of communication between French and British armies, were cleared.

When Humbert's army was established on the Lassigny Plateau, and the battle front on the Amiens salient subsided, Mangin, on Humbert's right, attacked between the Oise and the River Aisne at Soissons. Mangin began on 18th August with a local operation, which caused the Germans to withdraw their forward positions, but did not make the commander (von Boehn) send in his reserves.

On the 19th, therefore, Mangin extended his front of attack, and by the 20th had gained possession of the heights between the Oise and the Aisne. Thus Foch, in spite of no great numerical superiority, was able to attack successfully in convergent directions, leaving the enemy no time to recover.

As soon as Mangin had driven the enemy from the Aisne heights Byng's army began the battle of Bapaume.

Two of the three objectives which had been decided upon by the Generalissimo on 24th July had now been obtained, and up to this date 128,000 prisoners, over 2,000 guns and 13,000 machine guns had been captured since 15th July.

Now for the first time the enemy were showing definite signs of weakness, and decided on a general shortening of their front. They hoped to carry out their withdrawal in order to cause the maximum of delay and hardship. They wished to leave the Allies in the derelict old Somme battlefields while they were established in the intact villages to the east of it.

At this time the Hindenburg Line was nearer to our front between Albert and Arras than it was in the Somme valley. Haig proposed to upset their plan, to force them from the Somme uplands, and to turn the line of the river at Péronne southwards, by attacking from the Albert—Arras front through Bapaume.

The main task in this new battle was undertaken by the Third Army, which had to advance north of the River Ancre towards Bapaume, while the Fourth Army (Rawlinson) co-operated on its right by advancing astride the Somme on Péronne.

By the evening of the 21st the Third Army had gained the line of the Albert—Arras railway. On the 23rd a general attack on the whole front of the Third and Fourth Armies was made on the German defences north of the River Somme. These positions were captured with the Thiepval Ridge, Pozières, Courcelette, Martinpuich and Miraumont.

The effect of this was to raise our morale enormously. The German machine gunners fought with their usual courage. Our answer to their machine guns had been a hundred tanks supported by artillery sent forward to help the infantry.

By 20th August the progress of our Third Army in the north had begun to cause the enemy great anxiety for the safety of their troops between the Somme and the Oise. Accordingly, there was a retreat in this area, followed by our Fourth Army and the French armies under Debeney and Humbert.

By the night of 29th August the Fourth Army had reached the left bank of the River Somme opposite Péronne, while Debeney's army had passed through Nesle. Humbert then occupied Noyon. On this same day the Germans evacuated Bapaume, which the Third Army was gradually surrounding. As a result of these operations the Germans were driven completely from the Somme Plateau.

While the Third Army had been closing in on Bapaume the Australian Corps had been causing the Germans to withdraw up the River Somme towards Péronne. In the early hours of 31st August the 5th Australian Brigade, having crossed the river on improvised bridges and worked their way towards Mont St. Quentin, surprised the German defenders of that hill, which dominates Péronne, and carried it by assault.

As a result of this dashing operation the Australians were able to enter Péronne the following day, and the German defences along the Somme as far south as Ham were turned.

In the battle of Bapaume thirty-five German divisions had been driven in ten days across the scene of the struggle which in 1916 lasted from 1st July until 12th November, and in which they had lost 34,000 prisoners and 270 guns.

While the battle of Bapaume was in progress the Canadian Corps was transferred from the Amiens battlefield back to Arras. Here they captured the important hill of Monchy-le-Preux.

The First Army (Horne), to which these divisions belonged, followed up this success by driving the enemy back into the northern extensions of the Hindenburg Line. This Drocourt line had been completed by the enemy after the battle of Arras in April, 1917, and for eighteen months they had been improving it.

This part of the Hindenburg position, known as the Drocourt line, was assaulted in the morning of 2nd September by the 1st and 4th Canadian Divisions, and the 4th, 52nd, 57th and 63rd British Divisions, assisted by forty tanks.

These six divisions gained possession of the whole system of defence in less than seven hours.

On 3rd September Marshal Foch issued general orders outlining the plan upon which the fighting was to be developed. The Allied attacks, from the River Aisne to the River Scarpe, were developing successfully, and were driving the enemy back on the whole of this front.

In order to increase the pressure upon the enemy, it was necessary for (a) the British armies, supported on their right by the left of the French armies, to attack in the direction of St. Quentin—Cambrai; and (b) the centre of the French armies to continue to drive the enemy back beyond the River Aisne and the River Aislette, for the American armies to carry out the offensive already arranged in the Woeuvre as far as the line Vigneulles—Thiacourt—Regneville, and to make as strong an attack as possible in the direction of Mezières with their right protected by the Meuse and their left supported by an attack of the Fourth French Army.

The Generalissimo attributed particular importance to the Mezières attack, as the enemy were showing signs already of evacuating the St. Mihiel salient, in which case the American attack would be a blow in the air. Having given his orders for the front from the Scarpe to St. Mihiel, Foch turned his attention to the left of the line in Flanders, where there had already been much severe fighting.

It was proposed to take advantage of the exhaustion of the enemy, and of the fact that the fighting in France had drawn there the bulk of the hostile forces, to defeat the Germans in Belgium, and to reconquer the country north of the Lys. So, by breaking the hostile resistance and by gaining a starting point on the Clercken and Passchendaele Ridges it would be possible to cut the enemy's communications with the coast. By pushing forward to the Lys from Commines towards Ghent, any German reinforcements which might come from the south would be halted.

On 6th September the French occupied Ham on the River Somme and Chauny on the River Oise, and a few days later were within sight

D

of La Fere. With their right flank also threatened, the Germans south of Quéant had to withdraw to the outpost positions in front of their main defensive system.

By 6th September we had occupied Bailleul, Merville and Neuve Chapelle, while the 27th American Division had advanced beyond Kemmel Hill.

It may be well to compare the results of the two withdrawals by the enemy in 1917 and 1918:

Three months in 1917.—Prisoners, 21,000; guns, 220.

Twenty days in 1918 (21st August to 9th September).—Prisoners, 53,000; guns, 470.

On 12th September the American main attack was made by the I Corps of four divisions and the IV Corps of three divisions against the southern face of the salient, and was directed northwards in order to cut in east of the heights of the River Meuse.

Simultaneously, the V American Corps attacked with two divisions on the north-west front of the salient, and drove in eastwards the southern attack. One French division attacked on the left of the V Corps, and two more connected the V Corps round the point of the salient with the main attack.

The battle opened with a four-hour bombardment, and when the American infantry advanced they joined forces, and obliterated the salient with a loss to the enemy of 16,000 prisoners and 443 guns. This victory completed the preliminary attacks.

It was now seen that the great defensive system of the Germans no longer proved an obstacle to the Allies, and the enemy's trenches no longer prevented surprise or the concentration of superior numbers at the decisive point.

Foch's dictum was: "First stop the enemy, then continue to attack him at unexpected points. In the dykes there are weak places where the sea can come in and flood the land behind." Foch had carefully studied the German plan of attack and considered that they should have continued their offensive against the point of junction of the two Allied armies. Separation might have been fatal.

The German Command had made their attacks in divergent directions. The success of one battle did not influence any other.

On the other hand, when Foch attacked it was in convergent directions. Foch considered that any one of the Allied attacks under these conditions would produce decisive results.

If the "enemy is compelled to send all his available reserves to one part of the front, and when this has been done it begins elsewhere, and then again in a third place, the situation of the enemy is infernal."

For instance, on the Cambrai—St. Quentin front the British Third and Fourth Armies fought the battle of Epehy (forty miles east of Amiens), and drove back twenty German divisions, while the First French Army was driving the enemy back to the Hindenburg Line between St. Quentin and La Fère.

The Americans, during this time, were transferring troops from the St. Mihiel front to Verdun. This was done so secretly that the Germans had not reinforced their front in this area, where four divisions were overwhelmed by the nine American divisions.

On the evening of the 27th they had pressed forward seven miles to the southern slopes of Mont Baucon. A simultaneous attack was made in Champagne on a front of eighteen miles from west of the Argonne towards Reims.

By 1st October an advance had been made to the outskirts of Challerange, nine miles from its starting point.

Early on 27th September the IV, VI, XVII and Canadian Corps of the Third and First Armies advanced on the Cambrai front, stormed the strongly held Canal du Nord, advanced beyond Bourlon Wood and Fontaine-Notre Dame, and captured Sailly, more than six miles from their starting point.

Cambrai was then threatened from the north. The enemy, in order to rout these attacks west of the Meuse and at Cambrai, had taken troops and reserves from the seventeen miles of front from Voorme-zeele (four and a half miles south of Ypres) to Dixmude.

The Belgian Army, supported by some French divisions and by six divisions of the Second Army, attacked on the Voormezeele—Dixmude front.

This attack was carried forward beyond Passchendaele, and by the evening of 1st October had penetrated to the outskirts of Roulers. The Second Army drove the enemy across the Messines Ridge, cleared the Lys valley from Armentières to Commines, and reached a position within two miles of Menin.

Lille was now menaced from the north. This was followed by an attack on 29th September by the Fourth Army (Rawlinson) on a front of twelve miles. The First Army extended the battle front to the south, while two corps of our Third Army prolonged it as far as Marcoing in the St. Quentin Canal. The IX Corps attacked the St. Quentin Canal north of Bellenglise.

The men had life-belts and swam across the canal and stormed the enemy trenches on the eastern bank, capturing 4,000 prisoners and 70 guns.

On 30th September, and on the following days, the enemy was driven back on the whole front of the Fourth, Third and First Armies.

On the right of the Fourth Army the 1st British Division had by the 30th gained possession of the Le Tronquoy tunnel and crossed the canal to the north of St. Quentin.

The Germans on the following day retired from St. Quentin.

The Australians, passing through the Americans, went forward to within touch of the last line of the Hindenburg system, which ran through Beaurevoir (fifteen miles south of Cambrai).

The New Zealand troops and the 3rd British Division crossed the canal to the south of Cambrai, while the Canadians nearly encircled the town to the north.

By 3rd October the Fourth Army had broken through the Beaurevoir line, and by the 5th the whole line of the canal and the Hindenburg defences along it had been captured.

The result of these three attacks in Champagne, at Cambrai, and in Flanders was to cause the Germans to withdraw between Lens and Armentières. Everything showed that the enemy was in a state of considerable confusion and difficulty. Bulgaria had collapsed, and in the Balkans they were asking urgently for reinforcements.

Every day the American Army was increasing, and we had more guns, machine guns and ammunition than ever before. The great battle begun on 26th September decided the issue of the war. On 10th October Marshal Foch issued a general order that there were to be carried out three convergent attacks: (1) in Belgium; (2) Solesmes—Wassigny; (3) Aisne—Meuse.

Owing to the successes of the British armies this offensive would be continued, therefore, towards Mons and Avesnes (thirty miles apart) as well as (a) an operation to be carried out by troops (British) in combination with the Belgian attack, in a north-easterly direction between the Scheldt and the Sambre, so as to clear the Lille area; (b) an operation to be carried out by the First French Army in combination with the Aisne—Meuse offensive to outflank the line of the River Serre.

On 19th October the definite order for the advance of the Allied armies was issued. The group of armies in Flanders was to march towards Brussels; the British First, Third, Fourth and Fifth Armies south of the line Pecq—Lessines—Hal, with their right on Agimont (north of Givet, sixty-six miles south of Brussels), were to drive the enemy into the Ardennes. The First, Tenth, Fifth and Fourth French Armies, and the First American Army were to support the British attack on the left in the direction Capelle—Chimay—Givet, and were to reach the area Mezières—Sedan and the Upper Meuse.

The Germans now admitted their exhaustion and the possibility of not being able to continue the struggle. They were faced with the definite retreat of their Fourth Army on Roulers and towards Menin, and other successes compelled them to fall back by 15th October to the line Dixmude—Thourout—Ingelmunster—Courtrai.

The Germans now decided to shorten their line and retire on the Hermann line behind the canal at Eecloo and the River Lys. This involved the abandonment of the Flanders coast. This was accomplished by 17th October.

On 8th October there was heavy fighting, and the Second German Army was driven back towards Le Catelet and Bohain in the early days of October. This necessitated the Second and Eighteenth Armies being driven back into the Hermann line, as there were no reserves available in the vicinity. The Sixth and Seventeenth Armies were compelled also to withdraw behind the Scheldt into the Hermann line, as there were no reserves available in the vicinity; and by the 18th to evacuate Lille.

The Second and Eighteenth Armies were now included in the neighbouring armies. At this time the Germans, with 185 divisions on their western front, had seriously to consider their position. On 17th October, on the whole front west of the Meuse a rear line had been occupied, and on the right wing their retrograde movement was still in progress.

They got into touch with President Wilson with a view to the opening of negotiations. But while Ludendorff was actually pressing his views on the German Cabinet and appreciating the present military position, his new front was broken.

Their position along the River Selle was the connecting link between the River Scheldt and his line south of the River Oise.

The left flank of this position opposite Debeney's army rested on a series of very defensible wooded heights, which divided the valleys of the Selle and the Oise. On the front of the Fourth British Army the Germans held the eastern bank of the River Selle, and had occupied the line of the railway which connects Le Cateau and Solesmes.

This railway line ran through cuttings, providing the enemy with good cover and their machine guns with excellent positions. The River Selle had been dammed by the enemy, and was in flood, adding to its difficulties as an obstacle.

The battle of the River Selle began on 17th October with an attack by Debeney's First French Army, and the IX and II American and III Corps of the Fourth British Army against the German left from Le Cateau southwards.

After two days' hard fighting the Germans south of Le Cateau were forced back behind the Sambre and Oise Canal. The attack against the

German main position along the River Selle, west of Le Cateau, was made by a night attack with seven divisions of the Third Army and one of the First Army.

A mist in the valley increased the cover afforded by night, and enabled the infantry and engineers to lay foot bridges across the River Selle and to bring tanks down unseen into the valley. At 2 a.m. on 20th October the infantry advanced to the assault, and by 23rd October the Fourth, Third and First Armies made a general advance on a front of fifteen miles between the Sambre and Oise Canal and the Scheldt.

On the right the Germans were driven back into the Mormal Forest. In the centre our troops got to within a mile of Le Quesnoy, and on the left they approached Valenciennes.

In this battle we made a breach thirty-five miles wide and nearly six miles deep in their rallying line. Twenty-four British and two American divisions engaged and defeated thirty-one German divisions, and captured 20,000 prisoners and 475 guns.

On 14th October began an eight-day battle on the front from the River Meuse to Grandpré, where by incessant and hard fighting the Americans broke into the formidable German defences at many points.

On 16th October Grandpré was taken, while Gouraud on the American left stormed the heights about Vouziers and crossed the River Aisne. On the 16th, 17th and 18th there was a succession of strong attacks in which four divisions took part, which enabled the Americans to pierce the Kriemhilde line near its centre.

The Germans fought hard in this area, but the result obtained was that they exhausted their defensive power on the Meuse front just as Haig's attacks had exhausted it on the Cambrai—St. Quentin front. Also the American line was so straightened out as to be well placed for another general forward movement.

The German plan for a deliberate withdrawal to the Meuse depended on holding back the British on the River Selle and the Americans on the Kriemhilde line.

On 26th October Ludendorff resigned and left their Headquarters, as it seemed to him that there was no line on which the army could now stand. However, we were still far from their frontiers, and there were many strong natural barriers between our armies and the interior of Germany, and their armies if permitted to fall back on these would obtain a shorter and stronger battle front. It was therefore necessary to continue to press the enemy until his means of resistance, or his will to fight, was finally destroyed.

Another great combined attack was accordingly planned against the enemy.

Behind their centre, and blocking their way, lay the forests of the Ardennes and the River Meuse with its limited number of bridges. Their main exit lay north and south of the Ardennes.

The course of the River Meuse at Namur makes a sharp bend eastwards so that the German troops on the River Scheldt, on either side of Ghent, would, on reaching Namur, still have fifty miles to march and would find east of this town only four points of passage over the River Meuse.

If the British succeeded in crossing the Meuse between Namur and Dinant before the German forces in Belgium had got over the river, there was a probability that they would be driven against the Dutch frontier and forced to surrender.

It was essential therefore to retreat as early as possible, but to do this it was necessary to delay to the utmost the British and American progress. The plan now was for Gouraud and the Americans to strike for Mezières and Sedan, while the British armies made for Maubeuge and Mons, and threatened Namur before the Germans in Western Belgium could get away.

The French armies in the centre were to continue their role of harassing and delaying the German retreat, and the Belgian armies were to carry out the same role on the Scheldt.

The French troops on the Belgians' right, with two American divisions, were to assist the British advance by driving in the line of the River Scheldt and Oudenarde.

On 1st November the Franco-American attack began, with the intention of forcing the Germans out of the forest of Bourgogne by a combined advance from the east and the west. This was successful.

On the right of the American battle front their III Corps attacked in the River Meuse valley, while the V Corps broke through the remainder of the Kriemhilde line.

Simultaneously, Gouraud extended his hold on the heights on the eastern bank of the River Aisne opposite Vouziers.

The 2nd American Division made a *night* march through the German line for five miles, enabling them to shell Montmedy (thirty miles east of Vouziers) and Longuyon (ten miles south-east of Montmedy), through which the Crown Prince's army was trying to get away as much as possible of his war material.

The clearing of the Bourgogne Forest now enabled Gouraud to link up with the Americans, and to obtain a joint straight line east of the Aisne and Attigny (ten miles north-west of Vouziers), and to threaten the enemy in their Brunhilde line running from Attigny to Rethel (ten miles west of Attigny).

The enemy were then driven off the southern end of the Meuse—Aisne Canal, and were compelled to fall back from the Brunhilde line to avoid being cut off from Mezières.

Mezières was reached on the 10th, while the Americans had occupied Dun (ten miles south-west of Montmedy).

On the following days the III, II and XVII French Corps advanced through the wooded Meuse hills.

While these operations were being carried out, the British armies in the north were active. The Germans had now occupied a line from Ghent to a point two miles south of Valenciennes (fifty miles just west of south of Ghent), whence their front ran southwards to the River Sambre, which it reached a little above Landrecies.

It was considered necessary to get more ground for the advance between the Sambre and the Scheldt to force the enemy to fall back from positions between Valenciennes and the Condé Canal.

Accordingly, on 1st November, while the Americans were attacking on the Meuse—Argonne front, the XVII British and XXII Canadian Corps attacked south of Valenciennes and after two days' heavy fighting had, by the evening of 2nd November, turned the line of the River Scheldt from the south.

This gave the extra ground required for the attack, and enabled the Fourth, Third and First Armies to attack on a thirty-mile front from the Sambre Canal eight miles south of Mormal Forest to north of Valenciennes.

The British right had the difficult task of crossing the Sambre Canal and of forcing a way through Mormal Forest. This afforded the enemy opportunities for defence, and prevented the Fourth Army from making free use of its tanks. On the right the 1st and 32nd Divisions of the IX Corps fought their way across the canal near Cantillon, and by nightfall were three miles east of it.

The Germans were driven back into the Mormal Forest, and troops of the 25th Division of the XIII Corps, crossing the River Sambre, captured Landrecies at the south-east corner of the forest. North of Mormal Forest the 37th Division and the New Zealanders, after repulsing a heavy German counter-attack, drove the enemy back beyond the Valenciennes—Avesnes railway, and the New Zealanders, surrounding Le Quesnoy, compelled its garrison to surrender.

By the evening the left of the Third Army and the right of the First Army were on a front five miles beyond Valenciennes. On the British right the First French Army had also forced a crossing over the Sambre Canal to the north of Guise, and kept pace with the advance of the Fourth Army.

The resistance of the enemy was definitely broken and they never rallied. The three British armies captured 19,000 prisoners and 450 guns, and the First French Army took 5,000 prisoners.

South of Ghent the two French corps on the Belgian right, each with one American division, drove the Germans back along the River Scheldt, and the 91st American Division captured Oudenarde. The pursuit now was mainly delayed by the destruction of the roads and railways by the Germans.

On the 7th the Guards entered Bavai, and on the 8th the Fourth Army occupied Avesnes.

On the 9th the Guards and 62nd Division occupied Maubeuge, the French taking Hirson on the same day. Previously Tournai and Renaix were occupied in succession, and the 3rd Canadian Division entered Mons a few hours before the Armistice was signed.

The lines of communication immediately behind the German armies had been thrown into complete disorder, greatly intensified by attacks of the Allied airmen.

Our supply difficulties increased as we advanced, as the effects of the strain on railway systems in North-East France at this period were beginning to be serious.

During 1918 we had built or reconstructed 2,340 miles of broad-gauge and 1,348 miles of narrow-gauge railways, while to supplement the French rolling stock we sent to France 1,200 locomotives and 52,600 cars, but during the last four months of the war the weekly average load carried by the British military railways in France amounted to over half a million tons.

Apart altogether from enemy action, the mere lengthening of the lines of communication by the German retreat was a serious obstacle to our rapid advance. The enemy had also destroyed roads and railways, and made supply very difficult.

The advance of the British Army towards Germany did not begin until 17th November, six days after all fighting had ceased, and actually only sixteen British infantry divisions in France then moved forward. Again at the beginning of December it was necessary to stop the advance because the supply trains were running behind scheduled time. Also there was a large civilian population as well as released prisoners of war to be fed.

During six weeks we distributed five million rations among civilians, so that even if hostilities had been continued it would have been necessary to reorganize the supply services.

On the Lorraine front Foch had all his plans ready for an advance when hostilities ceased. The manœuvres preliminary to this advance had begun on 7th November when the three French corps immediately east of the Meuse attacked in the direction of Montmedy (twenty-five miles north of Verdun), a movement followed by the advance of the Second American Army through the Mœuvre towards Briey.

The left of the Second American Army had driven the Germans back some three miles in the Mœuvre by the morning of 11th November.

The general plan for this new attack was that the left of the Second American Army should be protected by the advance of the right of the First American Army, and of three French corps on Longnoy (fifteen miles north of Briey). These two attacks, which were to have been developed by 14th November, were intended to isolate Metz.

Thus, had the Armistice not been signed on 11th November, Marshal Foch had ready to launch between Metz and Strasbourg twenty French and six American divisions.

Had this attack taken place, the last line of the German communications would have been cut, and the German Army would have been completely cut off and at the mercy of superior forces on the front and flanks.

The will of the Commander-in-Chief had not only refused to admit defeat but it had compelled victory by the knowledge and skill combined with it.

Tribute must also be given to the Americans' energy and resource. In April there had been one division fit to take its place in the line; by 11th November twenty-four American divisions had been in action. They fought continuously on a front of twenty miles for fifty days, through line after line of German trenches, in a battle which entailed the employment of nearly three-quarters of a million troops.

As for our Army, it withstood for six weeks, from 21st March until the end of April, Germany's greatest effort. It was driven back at one point to a depth of forty miles. It lost 70,000 prisoners and 1,000 guns, and suffered 300,000 casualties, when fifty-five divisions were attacked by 102 German divisions, but it still presented a front which the enemy did not break.

Then, from 8th August, the British fought victoriously for three months, driving the enemy back 120 miles, taking more than twice as many prisoners and three times as many guns as they had lost. They completely routed the German armies on their front.

Germany, however, could not have been beaten in the field without the close co-operation of all the Allied armies co-ordinated for a common purpose.

CHAPTER VIII

SOLUTIONS TO QUESTIONS

QUESTION 1

THE effect of the great successes gained during the battles of the Hindenburg Line was not long in making itself felt. G.H.Q. was resolved to push the advantage gained to the utmost limit. Orders were issued on 5th October for a renewed attack by the Fourth and Third Armies to take place on the 8th, before the enemy should have time to rally and reorganize in a fresh position.

On the Fourth Army front the operation was entirely successful. The enemy offered a certain amount of opposition in the early stages of the advance near Brancourt and Serain, but before nightfall on 8th October the British troops had established themselves four miles to the east of their original position.

When operations were resumed early on the 9th it was clear that the Germans were everywhere in retreat, and the advance became more rapid. By the evening of the 10th, it had progressed as far as the general line of the River Selle from east of Bohain to just north of Le Cateau.

The enemy rallied behind this line of defence. Accordingly, the Fourth Army devoted the next few days to preparations for a renewal of the offensive on a large scale in co-operation with the French on its right and the Third Army on its left.

On the front of the Third Army, part of the Masnières—Beaurevoir line still remained to be captured. These last prepared German defences were assaulted on the early morning of 8th October along the whole front from north of Le Catelet to south of Cambrai.

Serious fighting took place particularly on the fronts of the V Corps on the right and of the XVII Corps on the left, the latter being subjected to a powerful German counter-attack aided by tanks, which checked its progress.

By nightfall, however, the whole of the Masnières—Beaurevoir line on the Third Army front had been captured, and the advanced troops had reached the line of the Cambrai—Bohain road, and had occupied the southern suburbs of Cambrai.

On the previous day the Canadian Corps of the First Army advanced its line to the north of this town, which was thus enveloped on three sides.

In the early hours of the 8th the enemy withdrew from its ruins, and, by the morning of the 9th, the Canadian XVII Corps were in possession.

The Germans during the next few days fell back rapidly to the line of the River Selle, which had been fixed by the High Command as their next position. Rearguards, left behind to check the pursuit, were driven in by British cavalry and advanced troops, and, by 12th October, the Third Army was once more in contact with the enemy's main forces along the line of the River Selle from the left of the Fourth Army north of Le Cateau to the Cambrai—Bavai road.

Meanwhile, to the north of the River Scarpe, the left wing of the First Army and the right of the Third Army forced the Germans to evacuate their defences covering Douai and the line of the Sensée and Haute Deule Canals.

The unequal resistance put up by the enemy gave clear proof that the spirit of their troops had been seriously affected by the defeats suffered in the battles for the Hindenburg Line, already described, and by the rapid progress made by the new series of operations undertaken by the Allies in Flanders.

On the evening of 13th October the VIII Corps was close to Douai and Arleux, while the XXII Corps connected the right of the Corps on the north of the river with the left of the Third Army, which was preparing, in conjunction with the Fourth Army, for a deliberate offensive against the River Selle line.

By this date the German Army's position had become very serious. In the centre they had been compelled to relinquish their hold on St. Gobain, and had to fall back through Laon towards Guise. The steady advance of the French and Americans on either side of the Argonne had forced their centre back between Reims and Verdun.

The further progress of this offensive threatened to lead to the envelopment and destruction of all the German forces between the Meuse and the sea.

The loss of the reserves at the disposal of the German Higher Command caused Ludendorff to withdraw and to shorten his front where it was possible.

It was for the Allies to forbid the enemy this final desperate resort by a resolute exploitation of all advantages gained by constant pressure on the tired and weakened German divisions at every point, and by vigorous blows on a large scale delivered wherever possible and with the least delay compatible with adequate preparation and methodical execution.

QUESTION 2

The objectives for the IX Corps for the battle of the River Selle comprised the capture of the whole ground between the Selle and the Sambre and Oise Canals.

The enemy must, if possible, prevent us from coming within artillery range of the railway junction at Aulnoye, the destruction of which by our guns would sever effectively their main lateral line of communication between Sedan and Lille. They must also gain time for carrying out the retirement of their troops in the Lens and Laon areas.

Only two railway lines were available, one along the coast to Etaples and Abbeville, and the other via St. Pol and Doullens, so that all movements from detraining stations had to take place during the hours of darkness.

The large majority of additional units, however, and formations, which were concentrated during the eight days prior to the attack were moved into the area by train. Altogether 230 trains for personnel and guns, as well as upwards of sixty special trains for ammunition, were run into the Fourth Army area, as well as supply trains for food and R.E. material.

The objectives of the day- and night-bombing squadrons were the railway centres Roye-Chaulnes, Nesle and Péronne.

Difficulties for the attack on 17th October were increased owing to railway congestion. Between 8th and 11th October the Fourth Army had covered an average distance of ten and a half miles on a seven-and-a-half-mile front, while the XIII Corps had advanced some thirteen or fourteen miles. The only main line of railway for supply ran through St. Quentin, Bohain and Busigny (fifteen miles north-east of St. Quentin).

The deciding factor for the rate at which the pursuit of the enemy could be carried out was the question of supply. The railway line between St. Quentin and Busigny had been reconstructed, but the periodic explosions of delayed-action mines made it necessary frequently to use railheads farther back. From these railheads the supplies and ammunition had to be brought up by motor transport.

QUESTION 3

A well-organized war machine is a powerful weapon when directed by the hands of capable leaders, but, when plans miscarry and days of difficulty and disaster have to be faced, it is the character and initiative of the individual, and that power over men which compels them to follow a commander, that are the dominating factors.

The war was in a great measure a fight to a finish between a marvellous war organization and a free people filled with pride of race. The campaign of 1918 was the final round of this titanic struggle, in which victory eventually went to the individual and not to the machine.

The moral effect of the Battle of Amiens was of the greatest importance. It demonstrated that the British forces had lost none of their fighting qualities, in spite of the reverses sustained in the enemy's March and April offensives. It proved that the British Army was as capable of carrying out a big offensive as it had been in 1916 and 1917, in spite of the heavy casualties it had suffered.

As a result of the fighting on 18th September the Australian Corps penetrated the enemy defences to an average depth of 5,000 yards on a front of four miles. All the strongly fortified localities in the old British line of resistance had fallen, and the captures amounted to 4,243 prisoners, 87 guns, over 300 machine guns, and 30 trench mortars.

The attacking strength of the 1st Australian Division was 2,854, and of the 4th Division 3,048, excluding the reserve brigades in both cases not engaged. The prisoners captured by the former amounted to 66 officers and 1,634 other ranks, as compared with 490 casualties, and by the latter to 99 officers and 2,444 other ranks as compared with 532 casualties.

These figures speak for themselves, and demonstrate not only the skill and gallantry displayed by the infantry, but also the moral effect of the tanks and the accuracy of the artillery and machine-gun support.

For the attack on the Hindenburg Line on 29th September we were undoubtedly faced with a very strong position; but all ranks realized the far-reaching issues of the result of the forthcoming attack, and, as on 8th August, there existed in the Army the will to conquer, and confidence in victory, that foreshadowed success.

The morale of our troops was continuing to rise every day with the consciousness of superiority over the enemy, and it was further increased by the arrival of the fresh British and American divisions which had reinforced the army since the 18th.

The Fourth Army had now been fighting for fifty-one days, driving the enemy from their positions. During this period it had employed nineteen divisions to defeat forty-one German divisions. The enemy's losses in prisoners alone since 8th August amounted to 46,500, including 1,100 officers, while our casualties in killed, wounded and missing reached 72,000.

It was estimated that the Fourth Army attack on the 29th would be opposed between Le Troquoy and Vendhuile by seven divisions, and that this line could be reinforced within seventy-two hours by six more divisions from reserve (actually eight divisions were met: 2nd, 8th, 11th, 54th, 75th Reserve, 79th Reserve, 121st and 285th Divisions), and six more (2nd Guard, 21st, 25th Reserve, 84th, 119th and 221st Divisions) joined in the battle within seventy-two hours.

The morale of the German troops after their severe defeats had undoubtedly much deteriorated, and would continue to do so with every fresh retirement.

By 16th October, on the eve of the battle of the River Selle, all arrangements had been completed. Patrolling had furnished us with full information as regards the state of the enemy's defences.

The morale of our troops had never been higher. They had, during the attacks of the 8th and 9th, seen the enemy in full flight, and they knew that there were no more prepared defence lines to be overcome.

Every day brought fresh news of the German retreat, both in the Laon and Lens areas. Optimists hoped that the war might end before Christmas.

On 29th October the 1st Division had established itself along the western bank of the Sambre and Oise Canal from Oisy to south of Catillon. In Flanders by the end of October the enemy had been forced back to the line of the River Scheldt, and the Third and First Armies had advanced our line well to the north and east of the Le Quesnoy—Valenciennes railway.

To the south the French had made progress. They had crossed the Serre and Peron Rivers, and had reached the southern bank of the Oise near Guise. In front of the Fourth Army the enemy was making a stand on the line of the Sambre and Oise Canal, and along the western edge of the Mormal Forest.

His troops, however, were depressed by continuous defeat, and were exhausted by incessant fighting, while the morale of our men was magnificent. The general attack was therefore delayed by the Commander-in-Chief only until such time as the preparations should be complete.

The victory of 4th November and following days finally broke the enemy's capacity for organized resistance. They no longer possessed the fighting qualities to stem the advance of victorious troops.

The morale of the great German Army had been shattered. In these circumstances the German nation had no option but to accept the terms of the Allies.

The Fourth Army general line was from Mt. Bliart and Sautain, through Martinsart Wood, round the eastern edge of Grandrien, along the River Thure to the western outskirts of Consolre.

Farther north the Third, First, Fifth and Second Armies reached the general line Marpent, east of Mons—Jurbise—Lessines—Grammont.

QUESTION 4

On 1st and 2nd November was fought the battle of Valenciennes: and then the Sambre battle.

By the growing weakness of the enemy in front of the British it was clear that one more rapid and resolute effort would be needed to consummate his defeat, and to force him to a widespread retirement, which would prove decisive to a campaign.

Orders were given by the Commander-in-Chief for a general advance by the Fourth, Third and First Armies towards Maubeuge— Mons, subject to the success of a preliminary operation on 2nd November against Valenciennes (five miles south-west of Conde), with the object of securing the right flank of the main offensive.

The minor attack was delivered at 5.15 a.m. on 1st November by four divisions of the XVII, XXII and Canadian Corps. The front of these troops extended for about six miles to south and inclusive of Valenciennes. Objectives included that town and the high ground beyond the course of the Lower Rhonelle River (runs two miles east of Le Quesnoy) (eight miles east of Valenciennes), a distance of three miles to the east of the starting line.

The operation was completely successful, though the enemy's resistance was so determined that it was not until 2nd November that all objectives were finally reached and held. This operation resulted in the capture of 2,500 prisoners, and successfully paved the way for the decisive operation of the Third and Fourth Armies two days later. It also rendered precarious the position of the Germans behind the line of the River Scheldt northwards from Valenciennes.

Preliminary operations were also necessary on the Fourth Army front, in order to clear the enemy from his last remaining positions on the west bank of the Sambre—Oise Canal. This was only partially completed, however, by 4th November, which was the date proposed for the general attack.

The Fourth Army operation orders enjoined an easterly advance on a front of fifteen miles to a depth of two miles, and an exploitation to within three miles of the Avesnes—Maubeuge (eight miles south-west of Le Cateau) road as laid down by G.H.Q.

The operation involved the passage of the Sambre—Oise Canal and of the River Sambre along the whole front, as well as a deep penetration by the right flank into rolling and enclosed country, and by the left into the depths of the dense Mormal Forest.

Most careful and detailed preparations were of first importance; various means of crossing the water obstacles were employed, including temporary and floating bridges, rafts, boats and even life-belts;

tanks were employed wherever possible, but a preliminary bombardment was dispensed with in order to ensure surprise.

The IX Corps on the right started the attack at 5.45 a.m. under cover of a heavy mist; its right and left wings at first met with sustained resistance around Fesmy (six miles south of Landrecies) and Ors (three miles west of Landrecies). The troops in the centre had an easier task after clearing Catillon (two and a half miles south-west of Landrecies), and were able to get well forward beyond the canal, thus facilitating the progress of their comrades, and by evening the Corps' front was roughly on the line Fesmy to south of Landrecies.

The XIII Corps on the left of the army achieved even more success. The passage of the River Sambre was forced north and south of Landrecies, and the town captured by an enveloping attack from three sides. Farther north the enemy was driven from his positions on the western edge of the Mormal Forest, and was forced to withdraw three miles.

The average progress amounted to between two and four miles, with the capture of 4,000 prisoners and 80 guns.

On the Third Army front the offensive was conducted by eight divisions in front and four in support. The objectives laid down for the V Corps on the right included the north part of the Mormal Forest, which in fact turned out to be a less formidable obstacle than had been expected.

Stubborn resistance was encountered, necessitating a whole day's fighting before the right of the Corps reached the open ground beyond the eastern edge of the great woodland. Neither on the left of the V Corps sector nor on that of the IV Corps was the forest quite cleared until late on 5th November. Farther north the New Zealand Division of the IV Corps accomplished a spectacular feat by scaling and storming the ramparts of Le Quesnoy (ten miles south of Valenciennes) after the garrison had been demoralized by outflanking movements on either side of the town.

The VI Corps on the left of the IV Corps had the hardest fighting of the day (4th November) near the Cambrai—Bavai (fifteen miles south-west of Mons) road. Its progress was less rapid than the others'. But, by the end of the day, all objectives had been gained.

On the XVII Corps front, the enemy fought half-heartedly, and, in spite of difficulties arising from the necessity of assembling the assaulting troops in the misty darkness of a November morning, all objectives were gained.

The XXII and Canadian Corps of the First Army were in action this day. On the right flank of the former corps hostile counter-attacks

E

compelled the relinquishment of high ground occupied early in the morning. Elsewhere the resistance was less serious, and progress was made.

The issue of the Sambre battle was decisive. Early on 5th November it was clear that the Germans were retreating along the whole front from Valenciennes to Nouvion Forest (just east of Oisy and Wassigny, seven miles south of Le Cateau), only resisting temporarily in the area just south of the Scheldt (*i.e.*, Mormal Forest and north-east of Landrecies) to secure the pivot of their rearward movements.

By nightfall on that day the whole of the Mormal Forest was in the hands of the British. Bavai was only a few miles beyond the line reached by the foremost troops, while British cavalry and airmen were following up along all the roads leading east and north-east the trail of the enemy's broken armies falling back towards Germany.

In the Sambre battle twenty-six British and thirty-two German divisions were engaged. The enemy lost 19,000 prisoners and 450 guns.

The clearing of Mormal Forest being completed, no large-scale engagements remain to be recorded. The Fourth Army organized a mixed detachment to follow up the enemy. The main body, owing to supply difficulties, was halted on the general line La Capella—Maubeuge (fifteen miles north and south of Landrecies)—Avesnes.

QUESTION 5

To the north of the River Scarpe the left wing of the First Army and the right of the Fifth Army, which had up to that date been held back well to the rear of the British troops farther south, undertook a series of operations which, beginning on 7th October, forced the Germans to evacuate one after the other their powerful defences covering Douai (fifteen miles north of Cambrai) and the line of the Sensée and Haute Deule Canals.

On the evening of 7th October (ten miles south of Cambrai) our advanced formations were just east of Masnieres (south-west of Cambrai), west of Cambrai and west of Arleux (ten miles north of Cambrai) and Douai—five miles west of Lille, to Commines (seven miles south-east of Ypres) and east of Moorslede, Roulers and Thourmont.

On the evening of 13th October the VIII Corps (Fifth Army) was closely menacing Douai and Arleux, while the XXII Corps (First Army) was preparing for a deliberate offensive against the River Selle line.

In Flanders the bad roads had necessitated a fortnight's pause in the exploitation of the successes gained at the end of September.

At 5.35 a.m. on 14th October, however, seven British divisions (X, XIX and II Corps) pushed forward to the attack on a ten-mile front between Commines and Moorslede.

The X and XIX Corps had as their objective the line of the River Lys as far as Welveghem (four miles west of Courtrai); farther north the II Corps by 16th October was able to reach and to secure the River Lys crossings on either side of Courtrai (fifteen miles east of Ypres).

The effect of this progress north and south of the salient held by the German Sixth Army in the Lille area was to render impossible the longer retention of that town.

On 15th October the German Sixth Army began to withdraw from the River Lys in the north to the River Scheldt in the south.

Lille fell to the XI Corps on 18th October (twenty miles south of Lille); the VIII Corps on its right had occupied Douai on the previous day, and crossed the line of the Sensée and Haute Deule Canals along its whole front. The XV Corps on the left cleared Roubaix and Turcoing (five miles and seven miles north of Lille).

Thus, the whole of the Fifth Army was engaged in a steady advance, which was only brought to an end, on 22nd October, before the line of the Scheldt between Valenciennes (twenty miles south-west of Mons) and Avelghem (twenty miles north-east of Lille).

Meanwhile, between 20th and 31st October the right of the Second Army reached Avelghem after heavy fighting on the II Corps front for the passages over the River Lys at Courtrai, and again on the 31st astride the railway from that town to Oudenarde (fifteen miles east of Courtrai).

This large-scale retirement of the German Fourth and Sixth Armies in Flanders and Artois had hardly begun before it was expedited by the important events in Picardy known as the battle of the River Selle (17th to 25th October).

In this battle the Fourth Army was to occupy the line Wassigny (twenty-five miles south-east of Cambrai) to Le Cateau (ten miles north of Wassigny) with the advanced guard pushed forward to the Sambre and Oise Canal. The Third Army was to occupy the line of the River Selle and its passages between Le Cateau and the Cambrai—Bavai (north of Mormal Forest) road. The First Army was to cover the left of the Third Army between that road and the River Scheldt.

On the Fourth Army front artillery preparation was undertaken from 12th October. The river 20 feet wide and 4 feet deep and everywhere commanded from the eastern bank, and also the railway between Wassigny and Le Cateau afforded strong defensive positions.

E1

However, this attack was to be carried out by IX, II U.S. and XIII Corps, having six divisions in line and two in support on a front of eleven miles, against twelve tired and weak divisions.

The attack started at 5.20 a.m. On the right the IX Corps had a difficult task. They gained their objectives, but the II U.S. Corps were short of theirs by nightfall. The XIII Corps, however, met the main difficulties.

Here the passage of the lower course of the River Selle and the town of Le Cateau had to be negotiated. The right wing could only cross the river at one part, and from there had to spread out to cover all the ground as far as the south of Le Cateau, which was to be turned by the left wing of the Corps passing the Selle on improvised bridges, north of the town.

This operation was carried out, and by the evening the whole of the XIII Corps was firmly established on the western bank of the river, and Le Cateau was captured. On the next day the IX and U.S. Corps carried their lines to within two miles of the Sambre—Oise Canal.

On the right the hostile resistance showed signs of weakening, but the Americans had to fight hard for their gains. On the XIII Corps front the plan was for the right to swing forward as far as Bazuel (three miles south of Le Cateau) in touch with the Americans, while the centre and left of the Corps remained stationary, facing north-east and in touch with the right of the Third Army.

This operation was successfully carried out, and by nightfall the enemy, broken everywhere along the whole army front, was falling back in haste behind the line of the canal. On 19th October British patrols were in touch with the new German position on the east bank of that obstacle.

Over 5,000 prisoners and 60 guns had been secured by the Fourth Army during the recent fighting, during the course of which fourteen of the enemy's divisions had been engaged and defeated.

The general offensive of the Third Army did not take place until 20th October, three days after that of the Fourth Army.

As early as 12th October attempts had been made on the fronts of the V and IV Corps to secure bridgeheads on the east of the River Selle between Le Cateau and Solesmes, but without any great success.

On the 20th the attack was resumed along the whole army front of nine miles, the VI and XIII Corps to the north and the V and IV also taking part in the fighting. The front of advance, in which seven divisions were engaged, thus extended from north of Le Cateau to the Cambrai—Bavai road (thirty miles north-east of Cambrai). The task before the army involved the passage of a wide river valley and the capture of high commanding ground, which had in parts been seriously prepared for defence. This was a difficult operation.

The day was wet and the mud was deep, but despite these adverse conditions tanks succeeded in crossing the River Selle and getting up to the assistance of the infantry, whose advance was in many places fiercely resisted.

The V and IV Corps, which began moving forward at 2 a.m., succeeded before daylight in establishing their lines firmly beyond the stream. By the evening the former had secured all its objectives, while the latter, in conjunction with the VI Corps on its left, enveloped and captured the village of Solesmes from three sides, and pushed on beyond it to its final objective beyond the line of the road from that place to Valenciennes (twenty miles north-east of Cambrai).

On the front of the VI Corps the line of this road had been secured, and despite repeated counter-attacks the XVIII Corps on the left flank of the army had gained the crests to the east of the River Selle. There it was in touch with the XXII Corps of the First Army, which had as its mission the security of the Third Army's left flank in the area of the Scheldt Canal.

This task was successfully accomplished by the occupation of the high ground overlooking the River Ecaillon and of Denain (eight miles west of Valenciennes) to the north of it.

Over 3,500 prisoners had fallen into the hands of the Third and First Armies during this day's operations.

After a pause of twenty-four hours, the general advance of the three British armies was resumed on 23rd October, the general objective being the attainment of the line Sambre—Oise Canal—Le Quesnoy (fifteen miles south of Valenciennes) to Valenciennes. This was a front of twenty-six miles.

The task of the Fourth Army was to secure and to hold a defensive front facing east to cover the continued advance of the Third and First Armies. The G.O.C. Fourth Army therefore determined to push forward to the general line Oisy—Englefontaine (ten miles south-east of Le Cateau and ten miles north of Oisy).

The attack was carried out by the IX and XIII Corps with four divisions in the line and four in support. Fierce resistance was encountered, particularly at Catillon (eight miles south-east of Le Cateau) and Bousies (three miles north-east of Le Cateau).

At the end of this action another 1,000 prisoners and 66 guns were left in our hands.

The main attack on this day, however, was delivered by the Third and First Armies between Mormal Forest and the River Scheldt, on which front the former army was engaged on a line of seven miles, and the latter on the remaining five miles. Nine divisions of the Third

Army took part in the advance, which continued during the whole of
23rd and 24th October; the remaining division of that army and two
divisions of the First Army came into action only on the second day
between the Cambrai—Bavai (forty miles north-east of Cambrai) road
and the Scheldt (runs past Ghent, Oudenarde, Tournai, Condé, Valenciennes to Mormal Forest).

After the first stage of the attack on the 23rd, when the enemy's
artillery fire was causing serious casualties, particularly in the area of
the IV and VI Corps, the infantry made good headway. The resistance
encountered was uneven; around Vendegies (ten miles south of
Valenciennes) the advance of the XIII Corps (Third Army: IV, V,
VI and XVII Corps) was checked until the afternoon of the 24th, and
a second-line division had to be brought up to effect its capture
against the southern wing of the army. Where the IV and VI Corps
were engaged the enemy fought with great pertinacity; whereas in the
centre the VI Corps made rapid progress, and before nightfall on the
23rd had advanced nearly five miles to the outskirts of Le Quesnoy
(nine miles east of Vendegies) and to the vicinity of the Avesnes—
Valenciennes railway.

Accordingly, a series of local operations were necessary during the
last days of October in order to secure the original objectives of the
advance as laid down by G.H.Q.

By the time these were completed the western edge of Mormal
Forest was in our hands, and also the whole of the Avesnes—Valenciennes railway from Le Quesnoy (exclusive) to within two miles of
the suburbs of Valenciennes.

In addition to this advance, the twenty-six Allied divisions engaged
in the Selle battle captured from the thirty-one German divisions
opposed to them 20,000 prisoners and 475 guns.

In the operations on the British front during October our casualties
had been some 120,000. In the area where the French and Americans
were fighting and advancing successfully, the Germans were in full
retreat to the line of the Meuse between Verdun and Mezières, having
lost their last prepared system along the Upper Aisne, while farther to
the west they were also withdrawing over open country from the line
of the River Serre towards Avesnes and Hirson.

The result of the Allied plan of advance was to drive the enemy
against the forest of the Ardennes, and so to compel him to carry out
any further retreat by widely separated routes; south of the forest
through the narrow valley of the Upper Meuse and north of it through
the defile of Liége.

The former gateway would certainly be closed by the advance of
the Allied right centre, and the attempt to pass all the northern
German Armies through the latter could only lead to inextricable
confusion and irretrievable disaster.

QUESTION 6

From the opening of the battle on 8th August to its conclusion the Fourth Army penetrated the enemy's defences to a maximum depth of twelve miles, forcing them to the borders of the old Somme battlefield, where there existed practically no accommodation for their reserve troops, and where the roads were exceedingly poor.

The result of the attack also influenced events as far south as the Oise. On 8th August the battle front lying between the Rivers Luce and Oise was held by the First and Fourth French Armies, whose sectors lay respectively north and south of Montdidier.

The moral effect of the Battle of Amiens demonstrated that the British forces had lost none of their fighting qualities in spite of the reverses sustained in the enemy's March and April offensives. It proved that the British Army was as capable of carrying out a big offensive as it had been in 1916 and 1917 in spite of the heavy casualties which it had suffered.

The G.O.C. Fourth Army had four corps under his command: the III Canadian and Australian Corps (twelve infantry divisions) and the Cavalry Corps (three divisions), 2,000 guns, 28 aircraft squadrons and 456 tanks between the Amiens—Roye road and the River Ancre opposed by two German armies (seven divisions in line and eight in rear). On this thirteen-mile front three objectives were assigned. The farthest was six to eight miles to the east of the starting line running through Harbonnières (six miles east of Villers Bretonneux) north and south.

The country was favourable for combined operations, being little shelled and open. The attack launched at 4.20 a.m. on 8th August overran the enemy's front-line system, and continued into his rear positions.

Along the whole front of attack to the south of the Somme all went well. The Cavalry Corps, with 156 tanks operating between the Roye road and the Chaulnes railway, was helped by the fact that a relief was just taking place in the sector of the enemy's line opposite the front of attack. The troops operating on the right wing of the Corps, however, were obliged at the commencement of their advance to debouch from a narrow bridgehead on the south bank of the River Luce.

This difficult operation delayed their progress, but they succeeded in reaching their second objective by noon. The final objective was not secured before nightfall.

Elsewhere on the Cavalry Corps front the line aimed at was everywhere reached, in spite of local resistance on the part of the enemy. The 1st Cavalry Division, passing through the infantry, rendered valuable service in the closing stages of the day's advance. The penetration of the enemy's line to a depth of eight miles and the capture of 6,000 prisoners and 160 guns were visible proof of success attained in this part of the field.

The four divisions of the Australian Corps on the Canadian Corps' left and south of the River Somme were opposed by three German divisions, and were considerably hampered in their progress by heavy flanking fire from the enemy's artillery north of the river.

Nevertheless, the infantry was on its second objective by 10 a.m., and had gained its final one shortly after midday. Cavalry and armoured cars came into action in the east, causing losses among the enemy's formations and among his supports advancing to the battlefield.

By 1.30 p.m. the Australian Corps had captured some 7,800 prisoners and 173 guns. Had there been a definite advance now, the III Corps might have made substantial gains on their front at points where they were held up. Pressure north of Moorcourt would have eased the situation at Sailly Lorette.

To the north of the River Somme the three divisions of the III Corps encountered great difficulties, and their success was proportionately less. Owing to local attack by the enemy on this front before the British attack was due to take place, it had been necessary to recast somewhat the original plan of operations at the last moment. The tanks allotted to assist the III Corps were unable to render full assistance to the infantry, and although ground was gained, especially on the left flank, it was found impossible to maintain all the positions in face of determined hostile counter-attacks.

Thus the III Corps by the end of the day, although it had taken 2,400 prisoners and 40 guns, had, on most of its front, advanced little beyond its first objective. The results of this brilliant day's work were, from the material point of view, of high importance, involving as they did the occupation of some fifty-six square miles of the enemy's territory, and the capture of 17,000 prisoners, 373 guns, several thousand machine guns and much material.

From the morale point of view the victory was important. Not only was the spirit of a considerable number of the enemy's divisions put out of action, but the enemy's High Command realized suddenly inevitable defeat.

QUESTION 7

Until 16th August the First French Army was under the orders of Field-Marshal Haig. At noon on that date it reverted to the command of the G.O.C. Armies of the North and North-East. On 17th August the Cavalry Corps was withdrawn from the Fourth Army, and the First French Army now operated on its front.

On 20th September it was decided after the success of the British on 18th September (Epehy battle) and of the American attack on the St. Mihiel salient on 13th September that four convergent and simultaneous offensives should be launched by the Allies. One was to be undertaken by the Americans west of the Meuse in the direction of Mezières, the second by the French west of the Argonne, in close conjunction with the American attack in the same direction, the third by the British on the St. Quentin—Cambrai front in the general direction of Maubeuge, and the fourth by the Belgian and Allied forces in Flanders in the direction of Ghent.

On the Fourth Army front on 29th September our total captures amounted to over 5,300, of whom 128 were officers from forty-eight battalions of twenty regiments of seven different divisions.

The American division had been compelled to face a very difficult proposition. Only the most self-sacrificing troops would have endured the fire to which they were subjected from the moment the attack started. It is to their undying credit that they broke the backbone of the tunnel defences.

On 17th October the American Corps co-operated with the Fourth Army, and, although opposed by the 3rd Naval and 204th Divisions, and by parts of the 24th and 243rd Divisions, after heavy fighting succeeded in driving the enemy out of the Arbre Guernon. They then held it in spite of vigorous attempts by the Germans to retake it.

QUESTION 8

On 8th August, of the four battalions of heavy tanks allotted to the Cavalry Corps each of the three leading divisions had one battalion. One battalion of tanks was allotted to the 4th Canadian Division to be employed in conveying forward Lewis-gun and machine-gun teams to the third objective. In spite of the difficulties caused by the lack of crossings over the River Luce and by the bad approaches to the bridges, the assembly of the troops and tanks was carried out without a hitch. At 4.20 a.m. the 2nd and 3rd Australian Divisions advanced. Each attacking brigade was allotted one company of twelve tanks and one supply tank loaded with ammunition and R.E. stores of all kinds.

The surprise was complete and the fog was so dense that the large garrison of Arroche Wood, which lay within the enemy's lines, was overwhelmed and driven by our barrage into its dug-outs, from which the enemy emerged only to surrender. The dangers resulting owing to fog from the infantry not being up with the barrage were neutralized by the work of the tanks, which, in attacking strong positions, enabled the infantry to capture them at small cost.

The 4th and 5th Australian Divisions each had thirty Mark V tanks and one and a half companies of Mark V Star tanks. They advanced at 8.20 a.m. to the second objective.

On 23rd August in the advance on Péronne by the Australian Corps, the 1st and 2nd Australian Brigades were each allotted twelve tanks and also three tanks of an older type to carry forward ammunition and supplies.

In the storming of the Hindenburg Line the Fourth Army was allotted the 3rd, 4th and 5th Tank Brigades and the 12th Armoured Car Battalion for the operations. Only a portion of the teams allotted were to be engaged on the first day of battle, as experience had shown the necessity of keeping a large reserve in hand for subsequent days' fighting.

The 4th Tank Brigade was to assist the American divisions to gain the first objective.

The employment of the 5th Tank Brigade except those held in Corps reserve was to be governed by the principle that each tank unit, in liaison with a definite body of infantry, should undertake a specific operation. On completion of their mission they were not to be attached to another formation without reference to the Australian Corps Headquarters.

The 5th Tank Brigade was allotted to the 5th Australian Division. On 1st October the tanks in helping the 5th Australian Division to capture Mill Ridge rendered great service, and later were able to capture Goncourt, but they could not reach the Beaurevoir (fifteen miles north of St. Quentin and ten miles east of Epehy) to Fensomme line (seven miles north-east of St. Quentin).

On 3rd October the Australian Corps attacked this latter line. The 5th Brigade had sixteen tanks, of which six arrived at the starting line in time. Delays were due to the darkness and the number of trenches, the shell-holes and the distance of 8,500 yards which they had to cover.

For the operations on 8th October the IX Corps was to advance on Fresnoy and Montbrehain and the II American Corps was to advance on Brancourt and Vaux. One company of Whippets was allotted to the IX Corps, two companies to the II American Corps and one battalion was to be in reserve. To the XIII Corps one company was allotted for the objective Estrées Maretz (six miles north of Bohain).

The Whippets were to follow close behind the infantry, and after the protective barrage had lifted off the line of the first objective they were to push on independently to the area of exploitation, beyond which they were not to proceed. The only serious opposition encountered was experienced by the 16th Brigade from the machine-gun fire in Mannequin Wood and the village of Mericourt. The Whippets of the 6th Tank Battalion supporting this attack broke down, and though the crews made very gallant efforts to repair them under fire, they were put out of action by hostile artillery fire.

In view of the unsuitability of the northern portion of the army front for tank action, the IX Corps was allotted the bulk of the tanks, two battalions operating with that corps while two battalions remained with the II and XIII Corps. The attack was continued at 5.20 a.m. on the 17th.

The unsuitability for tanks was owing to the nature of the hostile trenches and wire in the early stages of the attack. Therefore, the enemy's trenches were subjected to a heavy bombardment for forty-eight hours.

On this day an important part in the operations of the 50th Division was taken by the tanks. Of the twelve Mark V tanks allotted to the division, eleven were available, and these were distributed between the 151st and 149th Batteries, four tanks accompanying the right and left attacks, and three the centre. The only practicable place where they could cross the River Selle was where the St. Souplet (five miles south of Le Cateau) to Arbre Guernon road crosses the river. Here, where the stream was only eight feet wide and four feet deep, it was found that the crossing place could be effected with the help of cribs (strong hexagonal frames, constructed by the Tank Corps, which were dropped into the obstacles, over which the tanks then crossed). A route to the crossing place was taped out during the night and all the tanks arrived beyond the stream shortly after zero, and then followed up the infantry. Of the right group, one tank was bogged in the marshy ground, but the other three reached the first objective and mopped up several machine guns.

One tank of the centre group was put out of action owing to gas fumes, and the other two reached the first objective and became heavily engaged with machine guns.

Of the left group one tank was unable to cross the river, two were bogged, and the remaining tank, after overrunning two machine-gun posts, put out of action the detachments of two field guns near the orchards. It then proceeded to the vicinity of the station, where it disposed of two trench mortars, and then returned to St. Souplet station.

QUESTION 9A

By nightfall on 8th October, in the advance to Le Cateau, the enemy's disorganization was pronounced. They had used up seventy-three different battalions of thirty regiments of fifteen divisions, in addition to artillery and machine-gun units of two other divisions and companies of the 2nd Cyclist Brigade.

The G.O.C. Fourth Army ordered the offensive to be renewed at 5.20 a.m. on the 9th in conjunction with an advance of the British Third Army and the First French Army.

During the period of fighting from 8th to 21st August 23,064 prisoners and 400 guns of all calibres with many hundred machine guns and trench mortars had been captured.

In addition, large ammunition dumps, enormous quantities of engineering material, and a considerable amount of rolling stock were secured. Such losses naturally compelled the enemy to throw in reserves. These he could ill afford to spare in view of the wide extent of the Allied offensive, which at this time extended from Reims to Albert.

Prince Rupprecht's reserves, numbering thirty-six divisions early in July and destined for a big attack in the Ypres salient, were rapidly drawn into the battle.

On 16th August he retained only nine divisions in reserve available for employment between the sea and Albert.

From 20th July Rupprecht's reserves had been steadily withdrawn southwards, first to the Marne front to meet Mangin's offensive of 18th July, and later to the Somme to meet our attacks.

The battle of Mont St. Quentin (30th August to 2nd September) left the enemy in a very difficult position in front of the Fourth Army now that the line of the Somme had been turned.

The number of troops which had held the crossings over the river south of Péronne would not suffice to hold a position farther east without an obstacle such as the River Somme in front of them. This part of the front, which had been denuded of troops to provide reserves for the counter-attacks farther north, would have to be reinforced.

Nor was this all, for the Third Army had made rapid and consistent progress during the last few days and had carried its advance well beyond Bapaume. It appeared that, pivoting for the moment on the well-wired defences on the high ground about Nurlu (seven miles north-east of Péronne on the Péronne—Cambrai road), the enemy was continuing his retreat in front of the First and Third Armies, and that this retirement was to be followed later by a withdrawal in front of the Fourth Army and the French.

The G.O.C. Fourth Army therefore decided on 3rd September that an attack should be carried out to attempt to force a passage over the Somme by a surprise attack at St. Christ, and to open up the crossing at Brie.

By 6th October the capture of Beaurevoir (fifteen miles north of St. Quentin) was completed. Between that date and 29th September the enemy had launched no fewer than thirteen counter-attacks, and so had used up their reserves freely. It was significant, however, that they had without exception been engaged previously on several occasions since 8th August.

Not only had the enemy failed to prevent important strategical and tactical successes being gained by our troops, but he had suffered very heavy losses in men and material.

During the operations, which included the capture of the Hindenburg and Beaurevoir Lines, the Fourth Army had employed twelve divisions. The enemy had employed twenty different divisions, two of which were engaged twice.

The Fourth Army was still astride the junction of the Eighteenth and Second German Armies, hence reserves belonging to both armies could be brought against this army.

These reserves were estimated at fourteen divisions, all of which had previously been engaged, and were in various stages of exhaustion. No fresh reserves had been brought against the Fourth Army since 24th September, and the enemy could not easily reinforce this front by fresh divisions while the Allied forces continued to advance on the whole front from the Argonne to Flanders.

As a result of their failure to hold the Hindenburg defences against the British troops, the Germans were compelled to withdraw their forces along the whole front from Lens to Armentières.

QUESTION 9B

After the success of the British attacks on 18th September and of the American attack on the St. Mihiel salient on 12th September, it was decided between Foch and Haig that four convergent and simultaneous offensives should be launched by the Allies; namely, one by the Americans west of the Meuse in the direction of Mezières; one by the French west of the Argonne in conjunction with the American attack and in the same direction; the third by the British on the St. Quentin—Cambrai front towards Maubeuge; and the fourth by the Belgian and Allied forces in Flanders towards Ghent.

The most important and critical of these attacks were to be undertaken by the British against the Hindenburg Line.

F

On 2nd September orders were issued for our attack. On 22nd September the First Army was to capture Bourlon Wood, then to push forward and secure its left on the River Sensée and operate in order to protect the left of the Third Army.

The Third Army, against the general line Le Cateau—Solesmes, was to attack on the 27th with the First Army and press forward to secure the canal L'Escaut and to co-operate with the Fourth Army on the second day after zero day. The Third Army was to assist the Fourth Army with counter-battery work against the enemy in the region of La Tenière—Villers-Outréaux.

The Fourth Army, protected on its right flank by the First French Army, was to deliver the main attack against the enemy's defences from Le Tronquoy to Le Catelet, both inclusive, operating in the general line Bohain to Busigny.

Bombardment was to commence on zero day, and the assault was to take place two days after zero day, that is 29th September.

The Hindenburg position, of which the St. Quentin Canal and the Bellecourt and Le Tronquoy tunnels formed the chief features, was such that there could be no hope of rushing it, and behind it was the strong Le Catelet—Mauroy line well wired.

Rawlinson asked to attack it as early as possible after 11th September, as every day's respite given to the enemy was of value to them. The Fourth Army by this time was close up, and in the centre had occupied part of the old British reserve line of March, 1918.

Rawlinson considered that there should be the least possible delay for definite operations on the whole front of the army to gain possession of the outer defences of the Hindenburg Line. Such an operation, if carried out at an early date, would not give the enemy any opportunity of reorganizing his troops, improving his defences or becoming familiar with the scheme of defence.

Rawlinson did not consider that he could give a definite opinion as to the practicability of a direct attack on the main position until the high ground then held by the enemy at Holnon Wood, Le Verguier, and the high ground north of it, about Colopie Farm and the group of villages about Ronssoy and Epehy (twenty-five miles east of Albert), had been captured.

The possession of these advanced positions would give us good observation over the main Hindenburg Line, which was essential before an attack against it could be contemplated, and would enable reconnaissance to be made as to the best avenues of approach.

An attack on these advanced positions would be a test of the enemy's power of resistance, which was the ruling factor, and by the result of it we should discover the probable chances of success of an attack against the main Hindenburg Line. This attack was to be extended northwards by the Third Army and was to co-operate with the French to the south.

The French and Americans now had great difficulties of communications. This rendered advance slow, and gave the enemy time partially to recover.

The Third and First British Armies attacked on 27th September on a front of thirteen miles between Gouzeaucourt and the River Sensée, and took 10,000 prisoners.

On 28th September their advance was continued, and their troops established themselves on the east bank of the Canal de L'Escaut at Marcoing. The enemy, however, made most determined efforts to prevent the Third and First Armies from extending the bridgehead on either side of Cambrai.

The Canal de L'Escaut formed a very formidable obstacle, and rendered a further advance most difficult. That this would be so had been fully realized by G.H.Q., and the attack of the Fourth Army on 29th September was intended to turn the flank of the enemy's defences on the Third and Fourth Army fronts, and enable a general advance to be continued.

On 28th September the British, French and Belgians had also attacked between the River Lys and Dixmude, and had met with complete success.

Transport difficulties, however, as in the case of the Americans and French, prevented a rapid advance after their initial victory. It was estimated that the attack of the Fourth Army on the 29th could be opposed between Le Tronquoy (forty-five miles east of Amiens) and Vendhuile (ten miles north of Le Tronquoy) by seven divisions, and that this line could be reinforced within seventy-two hours by six divisions.

A serious drawback for the enemy to the Bellecourt tunnel defences was the fact that the high ground about Quennemont Farm, Gillemont Farm and the Knoll, when no longer in German possession, gave magnificent observation over them, and also provided the necessary cover for artillery to approach to close quarters for the purpose of dealing with the belts of wire that protected the defences.

Another weakness was the salient at Bellenglise, which, overlooked as it was from the high ground both to the south and north-west, was very vulnerable to the converging fire of artillery.

Further, owing to the configuration of the ground, it was difficult for the enemy, once the outer defences were lost, to find positions not under hostile observation, in which to place his artillery or to collect his reserves for counter-attack.

Behind the main Hindenburg Line there was only one single line
of trenches to arrest our progress. Another line, of which the wiring
was not complete, ran from Lessines to Le Catelet, passing west of
Magky-la-Fosse and Manroy. There was another line farther east,
namely, the Masnières—Beaurevoir—Fonsomme line. This, however,
was 5,000 to 6,000 yards away from the main Hindenburg Line, and
was too far distant to play any part in the defence of the canal.

QUESTION 10

On 8th November the dominant factor that decided the rate at
which the pursuit of the enemy could be carried out was the question
of supply. The main railway line between St. Quentin and Busigny
had been reconstructed, but the periodic explosions of delayed-action
mines frequently made it necessary to use railheads farther back, such
as Vermand, Bellecourt and Montigny Farm. From these railheads,
supplies and ammunition had to be carried up by motor transport.

The long distance involved the gradual breakdown of the roads as
the weather became worse and the traffic grew heavier, putting an
enormous strain on the motor transport. In several cases lorries were
on the road for seventy-two consecutive hours, and it was difficult for
the workshops to carry out the abnormal amount of repair rendered
necessary by the constant wear and tear and bad condition of the
roads.

In the forward area, where the roads had been destroyed by mine
craters, the infantry had outstripped the forward limit of lorries, and
it became necessary to use additional transport from ammunition
columns. It was quite obvious, therefore, that if the Army continued
to advance, complete breakdown in the supply organization must
result before long.

Consequently, on 9th November, Rawlinson decided that the corps
should be distributed in depth west of the main La Capelle—Avesnes
—Maubeuge road with an outpost line east of it.

QUESTION 11

In the River Scarpe battle we pressed forward ruthlessly. There was
no preliminary bombardment other than the normal harassing fire,
which was maintained until zero. The enemy, however, knew that
trouble was coming to them. This was proved by the statements of
prisoners, and also by the weight of the enemy's counter-preparation
during the night of 20th/21st August.

This bombardment was especially heavy at 4 a.m. on 22nd August, only forty-five minutes before zero, when a great quantity of gas shells were fired. The reasons for extending the front of attack northward to the area between the Somme and the Scarpe were that the enemy were not prepared to meet an attack in this direction, and, owing to the success of the Fourth Army, they occupied a salient of which the left flank was already threatened from the south.

The ground north of the River Ancre was not greatly damaged by shell fire, and was suitable for tanks. A successful attack between Albert and Arras in a south-easterly direction would turn the line of the River Somme south of Péronne, and gave every promise of far-reaching results.

It would be a step forward to the strategic objective St. Quentin—Cambrai. It was arranged that on the morning of 21st August a limited attack would be launched north of the River Ancre to gain the general line of the Arras—Albert railway, on which it was correctly assumed that the enemy's main line of resistance was sited.

The 22nd of August would then be used to get troops and guns into position on this front, and to bring forward the left of the Fourth Army between the Somme and the Ancre. The principal attack would be delivered on 23rd August by the Third Army and a division of the Fourth Army north of the River Somme: the rest of the Fourth Army was to assist by pushing forward south of the river to cover the flank of the main operation.

Then both armies were to advance and exploit any advantage gained.

The centre of gravity of the British offensive was consequently transferred for a time from the front of the Fourth Army to the Third Army north of Albert. At 4.55 a.m. Byng launched eight divisions against the enemy's defences between Grandecourt (five miles north of Albert) and Moyenneville (seven miles south of Arras) on a front of 16,000 yards.

Offensive operations then were to be resumed by the Fourth Army between the Somme and Albert on 22nd August as a preliminary to a general advance on Péronne. Although the enemy fought stubbornly against the Third Army north of Albert, the general condition of his troops along the whole of the Allied front was now known to be such that, if bold and resolute tactics were adopted, his collapse appeared probable. An order was therefore issued on 22nd August directing a strong offensive to defeat the German armies on this front.

For the next ten days the efforts of the Fourth Army were directed towards Péronne, in co-operation with the advance of the Third Army on Bapaume and with that of the First French Army on Ham. The troops of the Australian Corps, from the capture of Albert on

22nd August until they crossed the Canal du Nord on 4th September, covered a direct distance of fourteen miles over the old Somme battlefield.

QUESTION 12

CONCENTRATION OF SUPERIOR FORCE at the decisive time and place, and its ruthless employment in battle are essential for success.

Directly the enemy showed definite signs of weakness and decided on a general shortening of their front, Foch struck at the decisive time and place. They wished to leave us in the desert of the old Somme battlefield, while they established themselves in the villages east of it. As the Hindenburg Line was nearer to our front between Albert and Arras than it was in the Somme valley, so their plan of retreat was foiled by our advance on Bapaume.

In this battle beginning on 21st August the Third Army co-operated by advancing astride the Somme. The result was that their retreat did not economize troops and exhausted their reserves, with a loss of 34,000 prisoners and 270 guns.

On 12th September the St. Mihiel salient was obliterated with a loss to the enemy of 16,000 prisoners and 443 guns. The concentration was by seven American divisions attacking the south face of the salient in a northerly direction, in order to reach a position east of the heights of the River Meuse.

Simultaneously five army corps attacked with two divisions each on the north-west front of the salient, towards the southern attack. One French division attacked on the left of the V Corps, and two more connected the V Corps with the main attack. After a few hours' bombardment the American infantry advanced and joined forces.

By these concentrations of superior force the preliminary attack was successfully completed.

CO-OPERATION

Only by effective co-operation can the component parts of a fighting force act efficiently towards success.

By 26th August the progress of our Third Army on the north had begun to cause the enemy great anxiety for the safety of their troops between the Somme and the Oise, so these retreated, followed by our Fourth Army and the French armies under Debeney and Humbert.

By 3rd September, owing to the co-operation of all the armies, Foch issued general orders outlining the plan on which it would be possible to increase the pressure on the enemy, and without delay to make use of the whole forces of the Allies in converging directions on the most favourable parts of the front.

The Allied attacks had caused the enemy's retreat on the whole front from the River Aisne to the River Scarpe. Co-operation was to be continued by the British armies supported on their right by the left of the French armies attacking in the direction of St. Quentin—Cambrai; while the centre of the French armies continued to drive the enemy back beyond the Rivers Aisne and Aislette. The American armies were to clear the Paris—Metz railway by making as strong an attack as possible in the direction of Mezières, with their right protected by the Meuse and their left supported by an attack of the Fourth French Army.

Germany could not have been beaten in the field without the intimate co-operation of all the Allied armies co-ordinated for a common purpose with the full resources of the Allies. The British fought uninterruptedly and victoriously for three months, defeating ninety-nine divisions, regaining an area of eighty by seventy miles, and taking more than twice as many prisoners and three times as many guns as they had lost in the enemy's spring campaign.

MOBILITY implies the power to move and act with rapidity, and it is the chief means of inflicting surprise.

The long offensive on the Western Front exemplifies this principle. The first battle, beginning on 8th August, 1918, disengaged the Paris—Amiens railway and freed Amiens.

No sooner was the battle front on this salient at a standstill and Humbert's army was on the Lassigny Plateau, than Mangin opened an attack on Soissons on 18th August. As soon as he had gained the Aisne heights our Third Army began the battle of Bapaume, which went on to the end of the month.

Overlapping with this battle began the Arras battle, which ended on 3rd September by breaking the Drocourt—Quéant line. On 6th September the French occupied Ham and Chauny, and we occupied Bailleul and Neuve Chapelle.

On 12th September the American offensive began in the St. Mihiel region, followed by pressure in the Argonne country. All this time Generals Debeney and Mangin were advancing on our right. On 18th September began the battle for the Hindenburg Line. Epehy fell on this day, and the Canal du Nord was crossed on the 27th.

On the next day the Second Army, with the Belgians, forced the enemy from Ypres and advanced four miles on a twenty-two-mile front. On the 29th the Hindenburg Line battle developed into the Cambrai battles on a thirty-mile front from the Sensée to St. Quentin.

From 14th October the Americans were pressing hard on the front from the River Meuse to Grandpré, when our advance began in the Lys valley towards Courtrai, with our operations beyond Cambrai.

Thus by the full use of mobility the C.-in-C. had brought his armies in the first days of November to final victory.

OFFENSIVE ACTION

Victory can be won only as a result of offensive action.

By maintaining an offensive spirit throughout 1916 and 1917 our morale enabled us to withstand for six weeks, from 21st March until the end of April, 1918, Germany's greatest effort. We were driven back at one point to a depth of forty miles, but by continuous counter-attacks we were able to maintain a front, which the enemy could not break.

When, on 8th August, we took the offensive we were able to rout the German armies on our front.

Foch, by means of offensive action, eliminated the salients in our front, and obtained possession of the railways, which enabled him to gain the necessary mobility to concentrate his forces at the decisive time and place.

The final order for the Allied army to assume the offensive with convergent attacks on the 354-mile front was for the armies in Flanders to march towards Brussels. Our First, Third and Fifth Armies were to drive the enemy into the Ardennes. The First, Tenth, Fifth and Fourth French and the American Army were to turn the line of the River Aisne by advancing towards Chaumont-Porcisn, and on the right towards Buzancy-le-Chesne.

SURPRISE is the most effective and powerful weapon in war. By the night of 29th August the Fourth Army had reached the left bank of the River Somme opposite Péronne, while Debeney's army had passed through Nesle, Humbert's army had occupied Noyon, and the Third Army had been closing in on Bapaume.

On 31st August the 5th Australian Brigade, having crossed the river on improvised bridges and worked their way towards Mont St. Quentin, surprised the German defenders of that hill which dominates Péronne. By this fine feat of arms the enemy's defences along the Somme as far as Ham were turned.

By the evening of 2nd November, after two days' heavy fighting, the line of the River Scheldt from the south was turned and the Canadian Corps entered Valenciennes. This enabled the Fourth, Third and First Armies to attack on a fifty-mile front from the Sambre Canal, eight miles south of Mormal Forest, to north of Valenciennes.

Our right had the difficult task of crossing the Sambre Canal, and of forcing a way through the forest. Troops of the 25th Division of the X Corps crossed the River Sambre on rafts, surprised the enemy, and captured Landrecies at its south-east corner.

At the end of September the enemy, in order to meet our attacks west of the Meuse and at Cambrai, took their reserves from the seventeen miles of front from Voormezeele to Dixmude. We then surprised the enemy by attacking this weakened line and by overwhelming it with the Belgian Army, some French divisions and six divisions of the Second Army. By 1st October we had penetrated to the outskirts of Roulers.

The following are also examples during the 1914-18 war:

German gas attack at Ypres, April, 1915. The British tank attack at Cambrai, 20th November, 1917. The German attack, March, 1918, with no preliminary bombardment, and with their troops moving forward by night. Concentration of French Sixth Army north of Paris, September, 1914. French attacks in August and October, 1917, at Verdun and on the Chemin-des-Dames without preliminary bombardment. French defence of Reims in July, 1918, when the Germans shelled empty trenches. Allied attacks on 18th July and 8th August, 1918.

MAINTENANCE OF THE OBJECTIVE

Without it there can be no definite plan or co-ordination of effort.

In March, 1918, Ludendorff had a preponderance of 300,000 rifles on the Western Front, and an important and fresh reinforcement of trained men consisting of sixteen divisions and large quantities of heavy artillery.

Foch considered that they should have maintained their objective by continuing their offensive where it was first started, namely, against the point of junction of the two Allied armies.

Separation might have been irreparable. The Germans, however, made divergent attacks. Foch, on the other hand, maintained his objective, as when he attacked it was in a convergent direction. It was, therefore, sufficient for one of the Allied attacks to succeed to produce vital results.

From the middle of October the maintenance of the objective was fully achieved by the convergent attacks that were to take place (1) in Belgium, (2) Solesmes—Wassigny, and (3) Aisne—Meuse.

Owing to the successes of the B.E.F. this offensive was continued towards the line Mons—Avesnes. An operation was then to be carried out by our troops in combination with the Belgian attack, in a north-easterly direction between the Scheldt and the Sambre, in order to clear the Lille area. An operation was also carried out by the First French Army, combined with the Aisne—Meuse offensive, to outflank the line of the River Serre.

The main objective was thus continuously maintained until the enemy were forced to ask for an armistice on 11th November, 1918.

INDEX

76

79

The maps in this book are based on official maps appearing in the Official History of the Great War, Military Operations France and Belgium 1918, Vol. IV, with the permission of the Controller of H.M. Stationery Office.

Situation, 7th August, 1918.

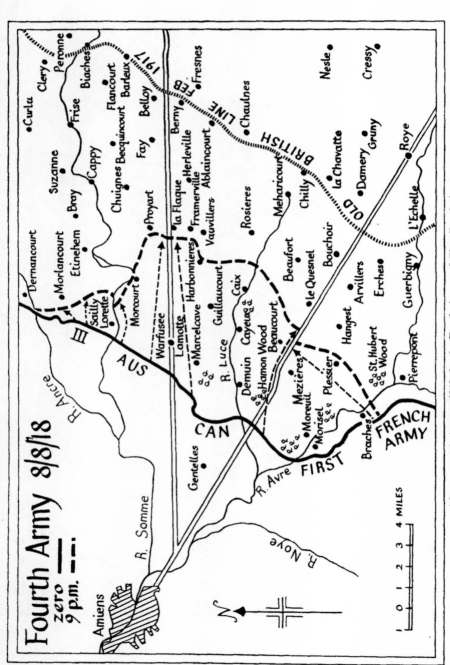

Advance on 8th August, 1918, by the Fourth Army and First French Army.

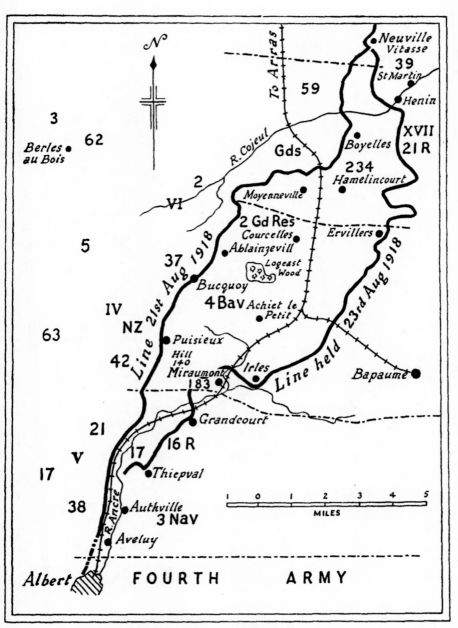

Advance of the Third Army, 21st to 23rd August, 1918.

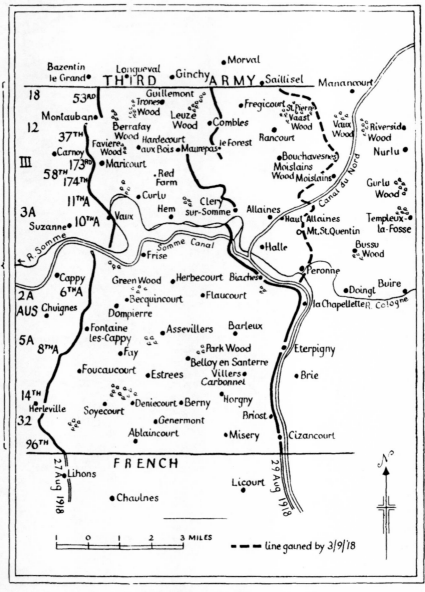

Fourth Army Advance, 27th to 29th August, 1918

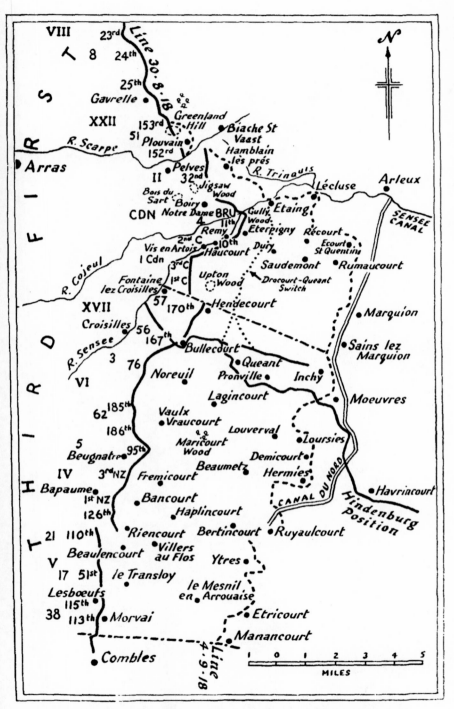

Advance, 30th August, 1918, to 4th September, 1918, by Third and First Armies.